The
East Texas
Sunday Drive
Book

The
East Texas
Sunday Drive
Book

By

BOB BOWMAN

Other Books By Bob Bowman

The 35 Best Ghost Towns in East Texas
(and 220 other towns we left behind)

If I Tell You A Hen Dips Snuff

I Ain't Sure I Understand Everything I Know About This

They Left No Monuments

The Best of East Texas

The Best of East Texas II

The Best of East Texas III

The Lufkin That Was

Say...Do You Know A Good Place To Eat?

This Was East Texas (out of print)

The Towns We Left Behind (out of print)

Land of The Little Angel, editor (out of print)

Second Printing, 1991

Best of East Texas Publishers
515 South First • P.O. Box 1647
Lufkin, Texas, 75901
Phone (409) 634-7444

Dedication

To my late father, Weldon, and my mother, Annie Mae Bowman,
and my in-laws, Oral and Catholine Shaddock
for their encouragement and support.

Table of Contents

Introduction

If I could reach back into time and resurrect a single forgotten pasttime, it would probably be Sunday Driving.

As a boy, I remember my father frequently telling our family on Sunday, "Let's go somewhere."

That was all we needed. With two adults and four kids squeezed into a Mercury sedan, we headed for a distant place on the map. It might be an area where our relatives lived. Occasionally it was a town where we had lived before. And sometimes we just went to a place where we had never been before. My father, though he was an automobile mechanic, never seemed to tire of driving.

As I look back on those Sunday trips, it has become increasingly apparent to me that few regions of Texas are as well-suited for the pasttime of Sunday Driving as East Texas with its abundance of forested scenery, an excellent network of country highways, and a wealth of history.

But, despite the advantages, many of us have given up the pleasures of Sunday Driving. Maybe it's the preoccupation we have with television. Or the increased demands placed on our weekend hours.

With this book, we hope to spur a renewed interest in the practice of Sunday Driving, especially in East Texas. Inside the pages, we've assembled 30 of what we feel are the best Sunday Drives in East Texas, covering a geographic area bordered by the Red River on the north, Interstate 10 between Houston and Beaumont on the South, Interstate 45 on the west, and the Louisiana state line on the east.

Each drive is designed to take about a half-day and averages about 120 miles in length. Most of the roads are designated state-maintained highways or city streets. The drives are divided into three sections: North East Texas, Central East Texas, and Deep East Texas. Each section contains about 10 recommended excursions.

In each Sunday Drive territory, we've tried to assemble some interesting facts about the towns and communities. You'll find the information heavy on the historical side because that's what we feel Sunday Driving is all about—learning more about our heritage. For good measure, we've thrown in some recommended eating places in case your Sunday Drive takes you through a meal time.

The maps accompanying each Sunday Drive were not intended to be complete. They are to be used as a general guide, and you may find it advisable to carry along a good Texas map. We also urge you to plan your Sunday Drive in advance, perhaps calling ahead to a local Chamber of Commerce or Tourist Bureau to check out opening hours and admission fees of some attractions.

Finally, one last piece of advice. Take it easy, don't worry about the time, and occasionally stop along the roadside to smell the flowers or listen to the birds. You'll be glad you did.

Bob Bowman
Lufkin, Texas

North East Texas

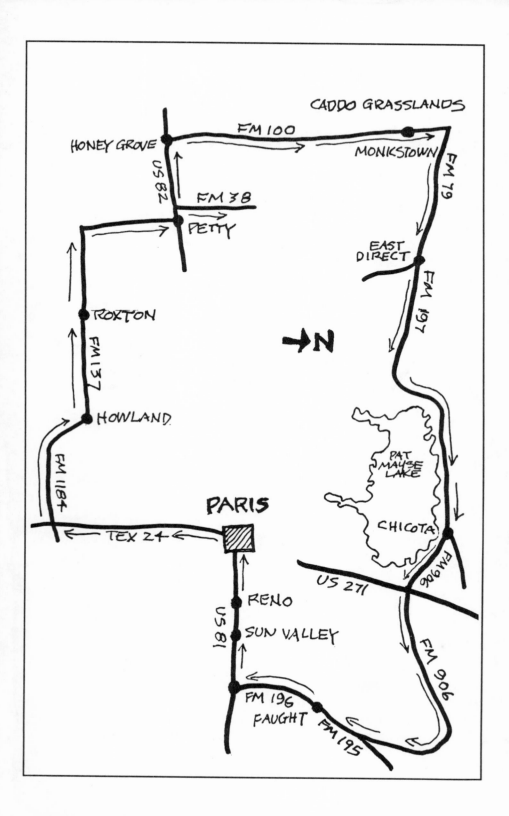

Paris:

Look for it just west of Blossom.

Here's a Sunday Drive that will carry you all the way to Paris (Texas, that is) and, at the same time, give you a look at some of the odd-named towns and communities that seem to characterize Northeast Texas.

For example, you'll be passing through places like East Direct, Blossom, Faught, Novice, Broadway Junction, Petty, Honey Grove and Monkstown, to name a few.

Start your tour at Paris, a town graced by dozens of beautiful old homes and unique public architecture.

Paris owes its name to Thomas Poteet, an employee of pioneer settler George Wright. Poteet suggested that the area where Wright and another family, the Chisums, had settled be called Paris in honor of his hometown, Paris, France. The Wrights and Chisums agreed and Paris eventually wound up as the county seat of Lamar County, which was carved from a portion of Red River County in the 1840s and named for Mirabeau B. Lamar, president of the Republic of Texas.

There's so much to see in Paris that you could spend your entire Sunday Drive here. One street, Church Street, certainly demands your attention.

Running in a north-south direction, the street includes some of the town's most imposing homes, including the Sam Bell Maxey Historic Structure at the corner of Church and Washington. Dating from 1868, the house was built in the high Victorian Italianate style and was the home for former Confederate general and U.S. Senator Sam Bell Maxey. The house is open for guided tours Wednesday through Sunday from 10 a.m. to 5 p.m.

Another imposing Church Street structure is the funeral parlor of Gene Roden & Sons, once the mansion of Paris businessman and mule trader Rufus Fenner Scott, who brought St. Louis architect J.L. Wees to Paris to design the home, which includes a three-story atrium and an elaborate underground drain system that allows the basement to remain dry.

In addition to Church Street, your Sunday Drive should take you along Pine Bluff Street, originally part of the Central National Road of the Republic of Texas, and downtown Paris, which features some of the most interesting business buildings in East Texas. Take time to walk around the downtown square and explore the architecture.

Other Paris highlights include:

• The burial site of John Chisum, the cattle baron whose life was immortalized by John Wayne in the movie, "Chisum." The old cattleman is buried in a cemetery in the 1100 block of West Washington Street. Chisum, a descendant of a pioneer Paris family, died in Eureka Springs, Ark., in 1884. Chisum earned the nickname of Jinglebob John when he cut the ears of his cows in a manner that left a part of the ears dangling, a practice known as a jinglebob.

• The Lamar County Courthouse, one block north of the town plaza on North Main Street. The building was rebuilt after the Paris fire of 1916 with the pink granite blocks that were salvaged and cleaned from the destroyed building.

• The Peristyle in Bywaters Park on South Main. It was also designed by J.L. Wees and follows the style of a Grecian temple. The Peristyle and surrounding park offer an appropriate setting for the Paris Municipal Band's summer concerts, a Paris tradition since 1923.

An excellent way to explore these and other Paris historical sites is to pick up a copy of the Paris Historical Guide at the local Chamber of Commerce.

To continue your Sunday Drive, leave Paris via Texas 24, heading south. At Broadway Junction, a few miles before you cross the Sulphur River, turn east on Farm Road 1184 and head for the Howland community. There, pick up Farm Road 137, which will carry you through Roxton and to Petty, intersecting with U.S. 82. Just west of Petty, take Farm Road 38 north and start looking for the signs to "The Back Side of Nowhere," an oddball country attraction with a railroad caboose, a berry patch, a swinging bridge and a fishing pond.

Return to 82 and travel a few miles to the west until you come to Honey Grove, named for its location in a grove of honey bee trees. Then veer in a northerly direction on Farm Road 100, which will carry you across the eastern side of the Caddo National Grassland.

Continue on 100 through Monkstown until you reach its intersection with Farm Road 79 in the Riverby settlement. Traveling east, you'll be passing through the farm and ranch country of the Red River. At the intersection of 79 and 197 in the East Direct settlement, turn onto 197 and continue in an easterly direction through Ragstown and Forest Chapel. You'll be passing along the northern shoreline of Pat Mayse Lake, which sprawls over some 6,000 acres along Sanders Creek, a tributary of the Red River. Several recreational roads leading south from 197 will carry you to the lake's shoreline.

Continuing on 197, you'll reach Chicota, named for an Indian word,

Checotah. Here, turn on Farm Road 906, which will take you across the lake's dam and to an excellent overlook area.

The farm road will eventually take you to Trout, where you should cross U.S. 271 and continue on 906 to the east. You'll pass through Lone Star and at Novice, you should pick up Farm Road 195 to Faught, named for a pioneer doctor. There, start south on Farm Road 196 to Blossom (originally called Blossom Prairie Depot), where you'll want to head west on U.S. 81, passing through Sun Valley and Reno before reaching Paris.

There are several excellent restaurants in Paris. We enjoyed John's Bake Shop on Clarksville Street.

(Additional information on the places included in this Sunday Drive may be obtained by contacting the Paris Chamber of Commerce, 1651 Clarksville Street, Paris, TX 75460, telephone 214/784-2501.)

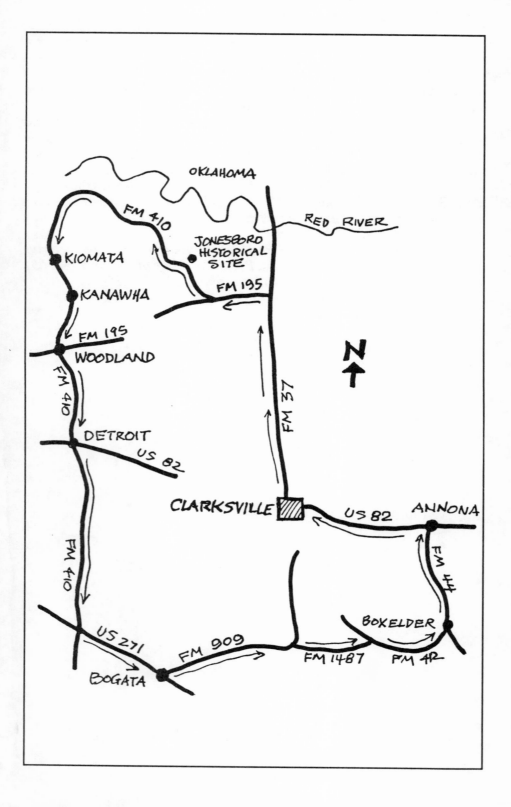

Clarksville:

Where the heritage is older than Texas.

The original Red River territory, which you'll explore on this Sunday Drive, was so large that 36 Texas counties were carved out of the vast region along the border with Oklahoma.

What is now Red River County had Anglo-American settlers as early as 1811. Stephen F. Austin visited this area before bringing his colony to Texas. And Sam Houston and Davy Crockett set foot on Texas soil for the first time when they crossed the Red River in the 1830s.

You should begin your Sunday Drive through the Red River county by starting on U.S. Highway 82 at Clarksville, a town older than the Republic of Texas, having been founded in the winter of 1833-34 by Captain James Clark.

The original county seat of Red River County was established at LaGrange, a community a few miles northeast of Clarksville. Within a few months, however, the county seat was moved to Clarksville and a two-room log cabin was built in the center of town on the square to serve as a courthouse.

The cabin was replaced by a brick courthouse, which was used until 1884 when Red River County officials built a new courthouse three blocks from the square. Instead of perishing from the loss, however, the square remained the center of activity for Clarksville and today still boasts many of the buildings from its earlier days.

A distinctive feature of the square is a row of seven two-story buildings, each the same height and general appearance. Four of the buildings have an identical architectural design and the three others also have a similar appearance. All seven apparently had the same architect.

There are so many historical landmarks in Clarksville that a history buff would have to spend days here. Here are some of the most prominent sites:

• The old square markers. A series of historical markers on the old town square tell the stories of Clarksville's role during the Civil War, the lifetime of pioneer preacher William Stevenson, and the importance of the stagecoach to the community.

• The home of Colonel Charles DeMorse, father of Texas journalism, located on the north side of 115 East Comanche. The site of DeMorse's pioneer newspaper, The Northern Standard, is located nearby.

• The Red River County Courthouse, whose castle-like features and imposing bell tower make it one of the most photographed courthouses in Texas

• The Red River County Jail, located on Madison Street. It was built in 1889 as a companion structure to the county courthouse.

• Clarksville Cemetery, located on the south side of blocks 600 and 700 of West Washington Street. The graveyard was first used in the 1830's for the family of James Clark, the founder of Clarksville and a veteran of the Texas Revolution. The earliest grave is that of his father, Benjamin, who fought in the American Revolution.

• The Hanging Tree, also known as Page's Oak, located at the northwest corner of the cemetery. It was used to dispense early justice in Red River County.

• The David G. Burnet Statue, located on the campus of Clarksville High School beside U.S. 82. Burnet was the provisional president of the Republic of Texas.

To continue your Sunday Drive, turn north on Texas 37. Just before you cross the Red River into Oklahoma, turn west on Farm Road 195. A few miles down the road, turn right on Farm Road 410, which will carry you through scenic pinelands, gently rolling farms and pastures, and the old plantations of the Red River country. Look out for an occasional plantation home; some are marked by crumbling barns, ramshackle homes and groves of pecan trees.

Beside 410, a few miles from its intersection with 195, is a small historical site bearing several monuments to old Jonesboro, one of the first points of entry for Anglo-American settlers. Named for ferryman Henry Jones, the town was founded around 1814.

The townsite and the territory around the Red River were claimed by both Mexico and the United States and in 1828-37 it was the county seat of Miller County, Arkansas. At the time it had nearly 2,500 residents.

Both Sam Houston and Davy Crockett entered Texas at Jonesboro in the 1830s when they became interested in the Texas Revolution. In 1836, however, Clarksville became the Red River District's capital and Jonesboro soon lost its trade and settlers.

At the historical site lies a tombstone to Jane Chandler Gill, an Englishwoman whose death in 1816 is remembered as one of the first Caucasian burials in Texas.

Continue on 410 and you'll pass through a couple of towns with Indian-like names, Kiomatia and Kanawha. Kiomatia, named for a river known as "clear water" by the Indians, has had a post office on and off during its career, dating back to 1816.

Kanawha was settled by a pioneer physician who named it for the Kanawha River in his native West Virginia. Boulware's Grocery at Kanawha is reminiscent of early-day stores found in East Texas.

At Woodland, 410 swings southward to Detroit, which lies at the intersection of 410 and U.S. 82. Here, you'll find an interesting row of turn-of-the-century buildings which have been converted into shops selling crafts, artwork, foods, and antiques. The town was named by a railroad agent for his home in Michigan.

Also at Detroit is the boyhood home of John Nance Garner, vice-president of the United States from 1933 to 1941. Garner's home can be found by turning south off U.S. 82 at any of the several convenient turns. When you come to the street at the east edge of the business area, turn south. The Garner home is nearby, partially hidden by trees. A historical marker stands out front.

Also at Detroit is the picturesque First Christian Church, built in 1902.

From Detroit, continue on 410, which will pass near the settlement of Fulbright. FM 410 will interect with U.S. 271, which will lead you into Bogata, one of the oldest settled Anglo-American towns in North Texas. William Humphries first named the town Maple Springs.

At Bogata, take Farm Road 909 and follow it until it intersects with Farm Road 1487, which will carry you to the intersection with Farm Road 412. This road will lead to Boxelder, named for a grove of trees. There, turn north on Farm Road 44 to Annona, where you should pick up U.S. 82 for the return trip into Clarksville. Annona was named in 1844 for an Indian girl.

The route from Detroit to Annona is one of the prettiest drive in the Red River region, passing through miles of dense pine forests and rolling meadows.

If you're on your Sunday Drive during lunchtime, we recommend Ted and Beth's Main Street Restaurant at Clarksville, which serves excellent homestyle meals and a superb hamburger.

(For additional information about places found on this Sunday Drive, contact the Clarksville Chamber of Commerce, 101 North Locust Street, Clarksville, TX 75426, telephone 214/427-2645.)

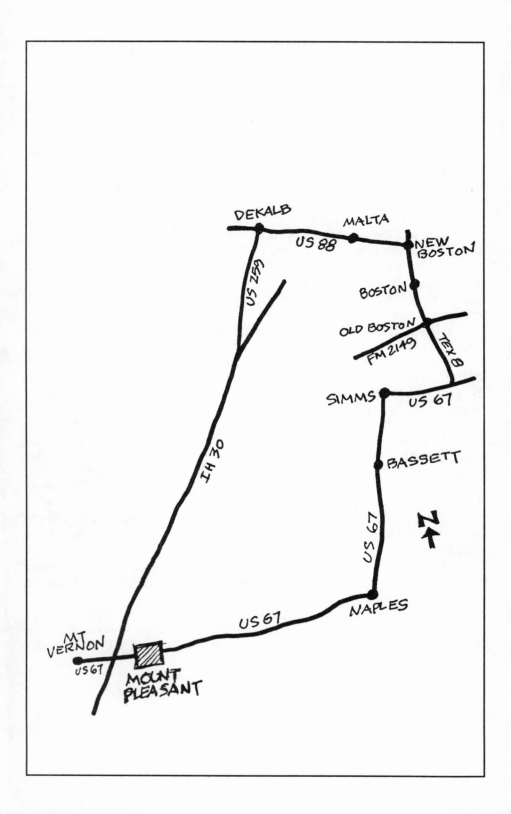

Mount Pleasant:
Naples, Omaha and Three Bostons.

If you're in the mood to visit cities you've never seen, but don't want to venture too far from home, here's a Sunday Drive that may help.

In one day, you can visit Omaha, Naples, Malta, Mount Vernon and Boston. In fact, you'll have the opportunity to visit three Bostons.

Let's start at Mount Pleasant. Founded in 1848, the town takes its name from a Caddo Indian legend surrounding a "pleasant mound" by red mineral springs in the forest. A pottery kiln established at Grey Rock in the southwestern corner of Titus County in 1864 later moved to Mount Pleasant, providing the town with a major industry and economic thrust. The town is the county seat of Titus County, which was founded in 1846 from parts of Red River and Bowie counties. The county took its name from A.J. Titus, a pioneer settler who fought in the Mexican War and served in the Texas Legislature.

Mount Pleasant has several interesting nature areas, including Tankersley Gardens, a five-acre setting carved from a creek bank, and the Bluebird Trail, a short scenic area of one of the most successful bluebird trails in the U.S.

Other attractions in the town include:

• The Florey-Meriwether Home, built in 1912 by W.H. Florey, the owner of the old Dellwood Resort Hotel.

• A downtown shopping district that includes antiques, fashions, and crafts.

• The Pleasant Jamboree, a toe-tapping musical held every Saturday night in the old Martin Theater, built in 1912.

• Three excellent bass-fishing lakes, Lake Bob Sandlin, Lake Cypress Springs, and Lake Monticello. The Bob Sandlin State Recreational Area is about 12 miles south of Mount Pleasant on Farm Road 127.

From Mount Pleasant, continue eastward on 67 to Naples, settled in 1879 and originally called Belder for an early settler.

From Naples, continue on 67 through the towns of Bassett and Sims. About 11 miles east of Simms, turn north on Texas 8. Here, within a few miles of each other, are Old Boston, Boston and New Boston, all located in Bowie County.

Bowie County was created in 1840 from a portion of Red River County, taking its name from Alamo hero James Bowie.

In the spring of 1841 the county picked the community of Boston as its county seat. The name came from W.J. Boston, an early storekeeper. However, when the railroad arrived in Bowie County in 1877, a depot was built about four miles north of Boston and was named New Boston. The first Boston became Old Boston.

In the early 1880s, the county's courthouse was moved to Texarkana, but a later election carried to move the county seat back to the geographic center of Bowie County. This location was between the two Bostons. The post office, adding to the confusion, named this location Boston, so Bowie County wound up with three Bostons.

A state historical marker at the intersection of Texas 8 and Farm Road 2149 can help you straighten out the confusion.

In Boston—New Boston, that is—take time to visit the James Bowie Memorial in the downtown area. New Boston is also famous for the Red River Army Depot and its annual Pioneer Days celebration each spring.

At New Boston, take U.S. 88 west to Malta, named by a pioneer settler for his hometown of Malta, Illinois. Proceed to DeKalb, the home of television western star Dan Blocker of Bonanza fame. DeKalb was settled in 1831 and named for Major General Johann DeKalb, a hero of the American Revolution who, upon the suggestion of Davy Crockett, stopped here enroute to the Alamo. The town was a county seat of Bowie County in 1840 and 1841. In the DeKalb region are several of the old hideouts of train robbers Sam Bass and Jesse James.

At DeKalb, turn south on U.S. 259. This will carry you to Interstate 30 and then back into Mount Pleasant, your starting place. A short side trip down U.S. 67 to the west will take you to Mount Vernon, another East Texas town with a famous name. While the town was named for George Washington's home, he never visited here. The town, however, is the home of former Dallas Cowboy quarterback and television sports personality Don Meredith.

The town is also the county seat of Franklin County. The county's picturesque courthouse, made of sandstone blocks, was completed in 1912.

(For additional information about places on this Sunday Drive, contact the Mount Pleasant Chamber of Commerce, 1604 North Jefferson, Mount Pleasant, TX 75455, telephone 214/572-8567, or the New Boston Chamber of Commerce, 109 North Ellis Street, New Boston, TX 75570, telephone 214/628-2581.)

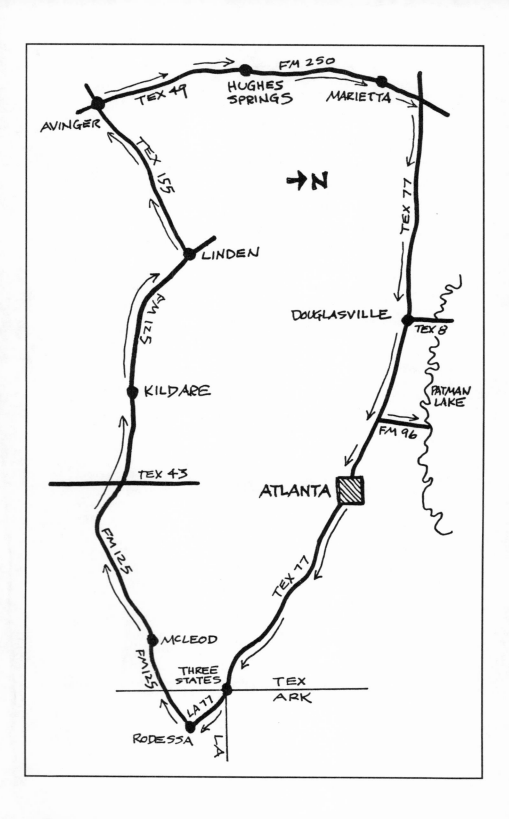

Atlanta:

Planting your feet in Three States.

This Sunday Drive enjoys a distinction few other drives in this book can match. It will give you an opportunity to visit three states in a single day.

Start your drive at Atlanta. The town, named for the Georgia city where many East Texans came from, was founded in 1872 with the arrival of the Texas and Pacific Railroad. The town's infatuation with its railroad history is reflected in the still-used Atlanta railroad depot and a bright yellow-and-red Union Pacific caboose in the downtown area.

Shoppers in the downtown area will find a hefty number of arts and crafts boutiques, an old-fashioned feed store by the railroad tracks, and some interesting business buildings.

On Louise Street, once a major thoroughfare for the city, are some of Atlanta's most interesting older homes, as well as an excellent city park carved from the side of a pine-clad hill.

From Atlanta, head in a southeasterly direction on Texas Highway 77. About 11 miles out of town, you'll be in Three States, the only place in East Texas where you can stand in three states at one time. Don't expect a flashy sign, however; Three States is pretty laid back with its reputation, and the only way you'll know you're standing in three states is to look for a U.S. geological survey marker resting under a large oak tree beside a local store.

From Three States, continue on 77 through the community of Rodessa, La., and a few miles south of the town, turn back to the west on Farm Road 125, which will carry you to McLeod, Texas, a town marked by its distinctive school building, a structure with an entrance faintly reminiscent of the Alamo.

From McLeod, continue on 125 through the pinelands, oil and gas fields, and ranching country of Cass County. You'll cross Texas 43 and pass through the settlement of Kildare, where the most noticeable structure in town is a large, two-story lodge building. The town was named for a railroad official.

From Kildare, continue west toward Linden on 125, a scenic route that stretches through the hilly pinelands.

Linden, the county seat of Cass County since 1852, boasts a courthouse dating back to 1859 and believed to be the oldest continuously-operated courthouse in Texas. The building's stucco front was put over the original brick facade after the building was damaged by fire in 1933.

Cass County was separated from Bowie County and organized in 1846, taking its name from U.S. Senator Lewis Cass of Michigan, a leader in the effort to annex Texas to the United States. However, Texans came to consider Cass' name an embarrassment during the Civil War and changed the county's name to Davis to honor Confederate President Jefferson Davis. The name was changed back to Cass after the war. Named for a town in Tennessee, Linden was founded in 1852.

From Linden, head in a southwest direction on Texas 155 to Avinger and then head north on Texas 49 to Hughes Springs, a town which had several prosperous foundries in the 1850s when iron ore was found in the county's red clay hills. The town was founded by Reece Hughes, an anti-secessionist who built a foundry but lost it when the Confederacy seized it during the Civil War.

Hughes Springs, Linden and Avinger collaborate each spring to stage the Texas Wildflower Trails Festival, usually in late April. During this period, you can see most of the wildflowers native to East Texas by driving along Texas 11 from Linden to Hughes Springs, State 49 from Hughes Springs to Avinger, and 155 from Avinger back to Linden.

To continue your Sunday Drive, pick up Farm Road 250 at Hughes Springs and proceed north through the settlement of Marietta to the intersection of 250 and Texas 77. Turn to the east again, motoring toward Douglasville.

A few miles north of Douglasville, straddling Texas Highway 8, is Wright Patman Lake, a 20,300-acre reservoir on the Sulphur River named for former Congressman Wright Patman of East Texas. You'll find several recreational areas off Highway 8.

From Douglasville, continue on Texas 77 until you reach the intersection of Farm Road 96, which will lead you into Atlanta State Park on the southern shoreline of Patman Lake. The 1,475-acre park includes facilities for swimming, boating, water skiing, fishing and hiking.

When you leave the park, return via 96 to Texas 77, which will carry you back into Atlanta.

(For additional information about places found on this Sunday Drive, contact the Atlanta Chamber of Commerce, 305 E. Hiram, 214/796-3296, the Linden Chamber of Commerce, 104 S. Main, 214/759-5741)

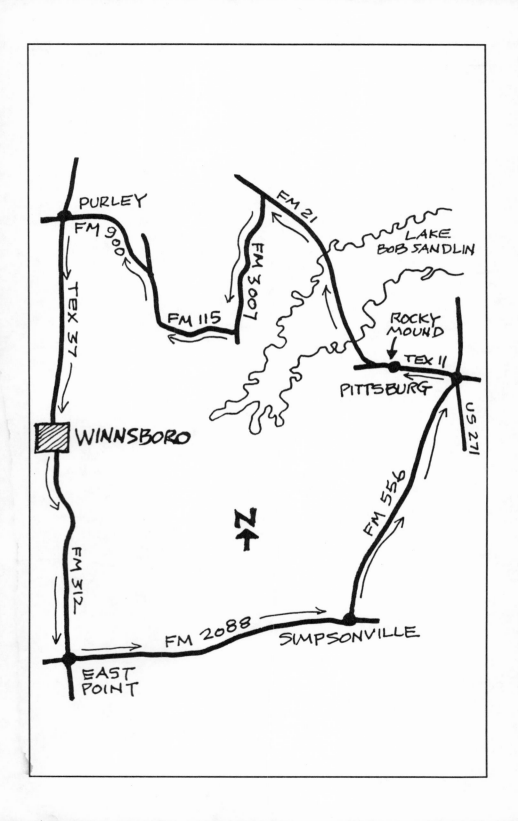

Winnsboro:
Airplanes, buttermilk pies, and autumn leaves

A Sunday Drive in the Winnsboro and Pittsburg area of East Texas will leave you with a different slant on aviation history, reward you with the best buttermilk pie in East Texas, and leave you dazzled by woodland scenery.

The area around Winnsboro is known for its autumn foliage, so the best time to make this Sunday Drive is in October when trees in the area start taking on hues of gold, yellow, red and purple. You'll want to pick up a tour map of the autumn trails from the Winnsboro Chamber of Commerce and you may want to time your drive to take advantage of the annual Autumn Trails Festival each October.

During your Sunday Drive, take some time to visit downtown Winnsboro. Some of the highlights include a restored railroad depot, a host of antique and crafts shops, and an excellent produce market.

Winnsboro was founded in 1854 as a trading center at the intersection of two main roads. In fact, the town's original name was Crossroads but was changed to Winnsboro to honor its founder, John E. Winn. In 1878, the arrival of the railroad brought growth and prosperity to the community and by the early 1900s the town was a leading center for farm products.

The town offers a number of special events during the year, including an antique car rally, a rodeo, chili cookoff, street art fair, fiddlers festival, trail rides, 10-K run and others. The Chamber of Commerce can help you with the dates.

From Winnsboro, head south on Farm Road 312 and when you reach the East Point community, turn east on FM 2088. Continue until you reach the Simpsonville community, where you should turn north on FM 556, which will carry you into Pittsburg—a town rich in East Texas folklore.

The town sprang up as a crossroads village in the 1840s, taking its name from Major William H. Pitts, who had come to Texas from Georgia. The community was later included in a new county, Camp County, which was created from a portion of Upshur County in 1875 and named for John

Lafayette Camp.

Known for its excellent spring peaches and hot links, Pittsburg also attracts attention with its replica of an airplane that the town contends was built and flown before the Wright Brothers flew at Kitty Hawk, North Carolina.

A year before the Wrights' achievements, Rev. Burrell Cannon, inspired by the Biblical passage about Ezekiel's flying wheels, flew an airplane into the skies over Pittsburg. A replica of the odd-shaped craft, called the Ezekiel Airship, now rests inside a downtown restaurant. A few blocks away is a state historical marker noting the achievement, as well as the old Pittsburg Machine Shop, where Rev. Cannon and his associates built the plane.

As surely as any building or person, the hot link has been tied to the history of Pittsburg. Originally brought to the town by Charlie Hasselback in 1897 as a delicacy for railroad workers, the hot link soon became famous in East Texas. Be sure to sample a few before leaving town.

Some other points of interest here include:

• Reeves Chapel Methodist Church, 4.5 miles southwest of Pittsburg on the Reeves Chapel Road, via FM 556 and 1519. The church, dating back to 1879, is one of the most beautiful in rural East Texas.

• The Abernathy House at 406 Quitman Street, a beautiful Queen Annie Victorian style home built in 1900 by a prominent Pittsburg dry-goods merchant.

• The Pittsburg Fire and Police Building at 132 Jefferson Street. This interesting building was completed in 1927 and sits on the site of the old Camp County courthouse. Sitting out front is the town's 1925 American LaFrance fire engine.

• The Pittsburg Gazette, 112 Quitman Street. Founded in 1884, it is the oldest business in town.

• The First Methodist Church, 200 Mt. Pleasant Street, noted for its prairie style architecture. The church dates back to 1857 and the present building was built around 1904.

From Pittsburg, head west on Texas 11. Near the Rocky Mound community, turn north on FM 21 across Lake Bob Sandlin. This 9,699-acre lake is the largest in a chain of three lakes in the Winnsboro-Pittsburg area. Several parks dot the lake and you may want to take time for a picnic.

Continuing on FM 21, you'll run into an intersection with FM 3007 north of the lake. Here, veer southward until you reach an intersection with FM 115. Take the northern route until you intersect with FM 900 at Purley, which will carry you to Texas 37. Head south back to Winnsboro.

There are several interesting places to eat during this Sunday Drive. Lou's Country Inn in Winnsboro is noted for its excellent country foods, including the best buttermilk pie in East Texas, and Gene Warrick has a couple of side-by-side eating places in downtown Pittsburg, the Hot Link Restaurant and Warrick's, home of the Ezekiel Airship Replica.

(For more information about the places found on this Sunday Drive, contact the Winnsboro Chamber of Commerce, 201 West Broadway, Winnsboro, TX 75494, telephone 214/342-3666, or the Camp County Chamber of Commerce, 202 Jefferson Street, Pittsburg, TX 75686, telephone 214/856-3442.)

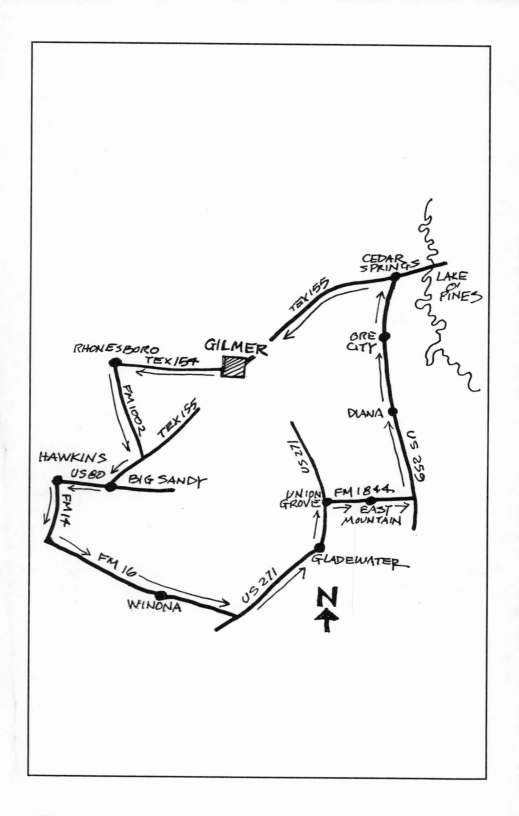

Gilmer:

Sweet potatoes, antiques and 'possums.

This Sunday Drive will carry you through three Texas capitals—towns known statewide for their yams, 'possums and antiques.

Start your drive at Gilmer, the county seat of Upshur County, where thousands of people turn out each October for the East Texas Yamboree, one of the oldest continuous festivals in Texas. It was started in 1935 when sweet potatoes were a major agricultural crop in Upshur County.

Events during the three-day festival include the crowning of a Queen Yam, a yam pie judging, a tater trot, the "tour de yam" bicycle tour and much more.

While you're in Gilmer, spend some time on the courthouse square, noted for the architecture of its buildings and its brick streets. You'll be delighted with one of the most attractive town squares in East Texas with dozens of small and interesting shops.

There are several historical markers on the courthouse lawn, including one detailing the history of the Cherokee Trace, used by Indians as early as the 1830s. The old trail is often marked in East Texas by the presence of small wilderness roses called the Cherokee roses. Indians supposedly planted the roses to mark the trail.

Gilmer and Upshur County, which were settled around 1835, owe their names to a couple of U.S. officials, Navy Secretary Thomas W. Gilmer and Secretary of State Able P. Upshur, who were killed in 1844 when a new Naval gun explored during a demonstration aboard a ship on the Potomac.

Gilmer has a wealth of old homes, including:

• The Gilmer log house, located at East Harrison and Cypress. The house is believed to have been built in the early 1840s.

• The Barnwell-Fowler mansion, near the corner of Montgomery and Buffalo streets. The house, containing 6,000 square feet, was built around 1913 and at the time was reportedly the strongest house west of the Mississippi River. With two stories and a basement, the house features walls of concrete and brick, 13 to 24 inches thick. All doors, because of their weight, have ball-bearing hinges.

From Gilmer, continue your Sunday Drive by heading west on Texas Highway 154 until you reach the small settlement of Rhonesboro, which bills itself as the Possum Capital of Texas. Frank Ford, who operates Rhonesboro's only grocery, maintains a small museum to "possumology" and the late 'possum expert, Spot Beard, who once said, "There are 14 different ways to cook 'possum...and 14 different ways to throw it out."

Rhonesboro has its own, tongue-in-cheek world festival to 'possums each year, and Frank Ford will be glad to give you his usual Chamber of Commerce pitch.

From Rhonesboro, turn south on Farm Road 1002 until it intersects with Texas 155 northeast of Big Sandy. Follow 155 into Big Sandy. Here, take the time to visit Annie's Tea Room, where waitresses in turn-of-the-century costumes serve fine country cuisine to the clink of delicate china and swish of fine lace. Big Sandy is also the home of Annie's Attic, a nationally-known mail order needlecraft company, and Annie's Bed and Breakfast with 13 guest rooms. In addition to Annie's collection of restored homes, there are several other restorations worth viewing in Big Sandy.

From Big Sandy, take U.S. 80 west to Hawkins, where you'll find the Hawkins Cafe, one of the last still-functioning oldtime cafes in East Texas. The meals are excellent and you'll enjoy rubbing elbows with Hawkins residents, who consider the cafe a regional institution.

From Hawkins, drive south on Farm Road 14 until it intersects with Farm Road 16. Turn to the east and follow 16 through Winona and then to U.S. 271. Follow 271 into Gladewater, a town that calls itself the antique capital of East Texas.

Dozens of antique and specialty shops line the streets of downtown Gladewater. But before you try to tackle the town, pick up a copy of a visitor's guide at the Chamber of Commerce. There are over 200 antique dealers and crafts shops within a four-block downtown area.

Gladewater owes its existence to the Texas and Pacific Railroad, which arrived here in 1873. The town was first known as St. Clair and stood at another location, but townspeople moved to the present location to be closer to the railroad line. The town's name was taken from its proximity to Glade Creek.

Like many towns in Gregg County, Gladewater prospered from the East Texas Oil Boom of the 1930s, but fell on hard times during the bust of the 1980s. Then Beth Bishop came along and started buying, renting and coaxing her friends to make use of the empty buildings downtown to house antique shops and malls.

Before leaving Gladewater, take time to visit Rosedale Cemetery, often called the world's richest cemetery. The site was started as a graveyard in 1854 when Sarah Armstrong was buried here by her husband, John Kettle Armstrong, who then donated the land as a cemetery. Two oil wells were drilled in the cemetery during the East Texas oil boom and have created enough wealth to make the cemetery one of the most attractive and well-kept in East Texas.

From Gladewater, continue north on 271, turning at Union Grove on Farm Road 1844. You'll reach the small settlement of East Mountain, home of the Old Country School, a 1930s school building which has been transformed into a mall for antique dealers and specialty sellers. Different artists and craftsmen are showcased on various weekends during the year, usually in June, September and November.

Leave East Mountain by continuing east on 1844. At its intersection with U.S. 259, turn north on 259, traveling through the communities of Diana, Ore City and Cedar Springs. At Cedar Springs, turn east on Texas 155 toward Lake O' The Pines, an 18,700-acre reservoir known as one of the most attractive lakes in East Texas. Here, you'll find several lakeside recreational areas.

Return to 155 and head west toward Gilmer. Enroute, be sure to stop at Barnwell Mountain Roadside Park. It sits atop one of the highest overlooks in East Texas and offers an unobstructed view of the country-side.

(For additional information about places found on this Sunday Drive, contact the Upshur County Chamber of Commerce, Box 854, Gilmer, TX 75644, telephone 214/843-2413, or the Gladewater Chamber of Commerce, 215 North Main Street, Gladewater, TX 75647, telephone 214/845-2626.)

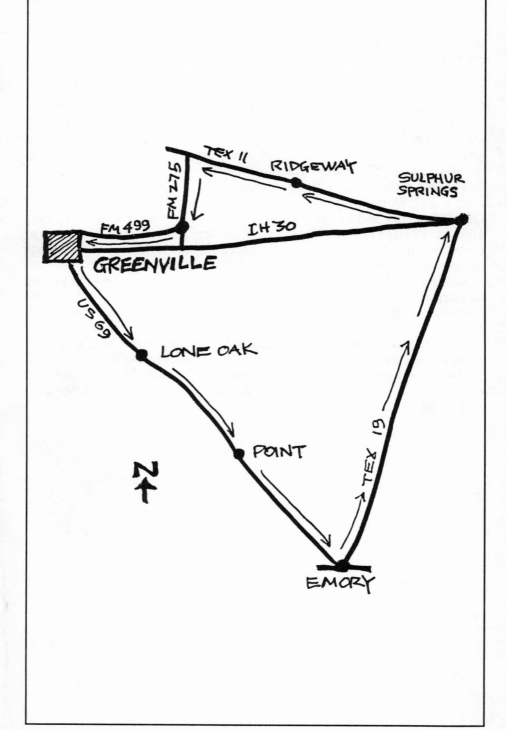

Greenville:

The story of two downtown Revivals.

While you'll see some pleasant East Texas countryside, this Sunday Drive is really designed to give you a look at the downtown revivals taking place in a couple of small cities, Greenville and Sulphur Springs.

Start your Sunday Drive by spending some time in downtown Greenville, which, like many other small towns in East Texas, is trying to breath life back into its traditional downtown region with a mixture of history, boutique shopping and professional firms.

Greenville's history dates back to 1846 when the town was chosen the county seat for Hunt County by one vote over Center Point. Named for General Thomas Green, the town eventually became the center of a cotton-producing area and at one time had one of the world's largest inland cotton compresses.

One of the most interesting structures in town is the downtown Central Christian Church, an outstanding example of Gothic revival architecture, at the corner of Washington and Wesley. The building—resplendent with its stained glass windows, grill-like brickwork, and interesting towers—was built in 1879 at a cost of $23,000 and restored in 1986 at a cost of many thousands more.

Downtown Greenville has a number of other turn-of-the-century buildings, an active arts and crafts community, and is a good starting place for traveling down Park Street, home of some of the town's most attractive historic houses.

Park Street will also carry you out of town via U.S. 69 toward Emory. Enroute you'll cross the Sabine River, which originates in the rural countryside around Greenville. Before its rush into the Gulf of Mexico several hundred miles southward, the Sabine becomes one of Texas' largest and most powerful rivers.

U.S. 69 will carry you through Lone Oak, where the most interesting sight in town is an abandoned but scenic cotton gin surrounded by old automobiles. It's worth at least a quick look.

At Emory, turn off the main road and spend a few minutes on the square of the yellow-domed Rains County courthouse. Around the vicinity of the courthouse square is the First National Bank, a typical early-day bank of the kind that Bonnie and Clyde often robbed. A few blocks away is the rockhouse home of Tony's Used Cars, an interesting contrast in architecture.

A few miles out of town on 69, pull over to the side of the road and read the historical marker to Fraser Brick Company, the first industrial plant in Rains County. The old plant stood in the settlement of Ginger, which took its name from the distinctive color of burnt-clay brick produced by Walter B. Fraser's pioneer factory.

Emory is unique in that it owes both its name and the county's name to a single individual, Emory Rains, who settled east of the townsite in 1848. Emory was originally named Springfield but was renamed when the county was founded in 1870.

From Emory, turn in a northerly direction on Texas 19, heading for Sulphur Springs, where you'll want to spend some time. Among the attractions here are:

• The Hopkins County courthouse, designed by architect James R. Gordon and completed in 1895. The three-story masterpiece, constructed of red granite with contrasting sandstone, is one of the most photographed buildings in East Texas.

• Heritage Square, completed in 1987, has restored to the downtown square the green space and park activity reminiscent of the town's early history. The fountain is fed from an underground spring.

• The Hopkins County Museum and Heritage Park, sprawling over 11 acres, is home for a growing number of original historic houses, shops and mills moved to the site, including the county's oldest brick structure, the 1870-circa Atkins House. The park is located at 416 North Jackson Street.

• The Music Box Gallery, located on the second floor of the City Library at 201 North Davis Street, contains the most unique and largest collection of music boxes in the country.

• It's appropriate that Sulphur Springs, which calls itself the dairy capital of Texas, should have the only museum in the Southwest devoted to the dairy industry. The museum includes a horse-drawn milk wagon, an assortments of churns, butter and ice cream molds, vintage photographs, old cheese-making equipment, and other relics.

Sulphur Springs was founded originally as Bright Star in the 1850s when stores and a hotel became a popular camping place for teamsters hauling goods west from Jefferson. The town changed its name in 1871 when mineral springs in the area were being advertised to make the town a health resort.

From Sulphur Springs, hop on Interstate 30 for a quick trip back to Greenville. Or if you prefer a more leisurely, scenic excursion, take Texas 11 out of Sulphur Springs through Ridgeway until you reach its intersection with Farm Road 275. Follow 275 south until you intersect with Farm Road 499 at Cumby. Then continue on 499, passing through Campbell, until you reach Greenville.

If you become hungry during the Sunday Drive, we recommend The Spare Rib, a Greenville barbecue place on Texas Highway 34, just south of Interstate 30. It has been in business nearly 40 years, and the barbecue is among the best in East Texas.

(For more information about the places found on this Sunday Drive, contact the Greenville Chamber of Commerce, 2713 Stonewall, Greenville, TX 75401, telephone 214/455-1510.)

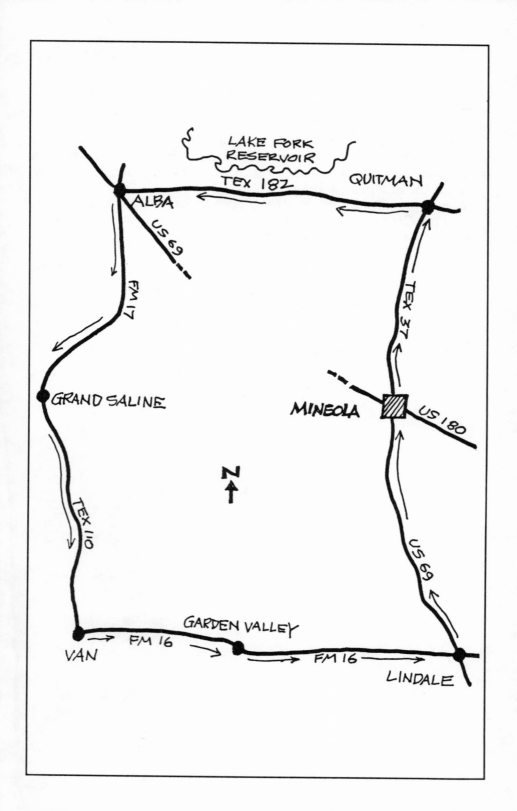

Mineola:

Lunch in a hardware store.

This Sunday Drive begins at Mineola, a town established in the early 1840s when Texas was still new to statehood. However, the town wasn't called Mineola until 1873 when it was officially chartered.

The town has an excellent historic district worth a walking tour. It includes a railroad museum (a former depot), a farmer's market where you can buy fresh produce in season, several excellent bed-and-breakfast inns, a host of arts and crafts stores, and an ample supply of restaurants. The district lies adjacent to the town's railroad tracks, which were first put down in 1873 with the arrival of the International Great Northern and Texas Pacific Railroad.

A number of historic buildings of brick and stone still stand in the downtown area and the town has an excellent community playhouse, the Lake Country Playhouse, which stages six shows a year in a former movie theater in the downtown district.

A good example of how Mineola has revitalized its downtown area is Kitchens Hardware and Deli. Housed in an old hardware store built in 1899, the store offers an interesting mix of hardware, gifts, and meals.

Mineola is also the home of a distinctly rural radio station, KMOO.

To continue your Sunday drive, head out of Mineola on Texas 37 for a pleasant 10-mile drive to Quitman, the county seat of Wood County. Here, you'll find several points of interest, including:

• The Governor Hogg Shrine State Park and Museum within the town's city limits. This is the home of Texas' first native-born governor. The museum has hundreds of momentoes of Gov. James Stephen Hogg's service and early life in Wood County. Picnic facilities are also available in the park.

• The Miss Ima Hogg Museum, also located in the same park, along with the Colonel James A. Stinson home, which has been restored to its early glory.

• The park is the home of the annual Old Settlers Reunion, perhaps the oldest active annual reunion in East Texas. It has been held in Quitman every year since 1902, except for two years during World War II. The Old

Settlers Reunion Tabernacle still stands in the park, although it was restored and enlarged in 1969.

• The Wood County Courthouse, built in 1850 on the south side of the town's public square.

Quitman, named for an early governor of Mississippi, is also famous for its dogwoods and each spring, from late March to early April, the town stages its annual Quitman Dogwood Fiesta featuring dogwood tours, an arts and crafts show, a parade, style show, trail ride, street dance and other activities.

From Quitman, travel westward on Texas 182 to Alba, which has one of the most interesting histories in Wood County. The town was settled about 1860 and was said to have been intended for white settlers only; hence the name Alba. One of the first settlers was Josh Wilson, who came to Texas from Arkansas. In 1882, the town became a stop on the Missouri, Kansas and Texas Railroad.

Enroute from Quitman to Alba, you'll pass the 12,600-foot long earthen dam for Lake Fork Reservoir with a surface of about 27,000 acres. An excellent place to look over the lake is at the Sabine River Authority's administration grounds, which can be reached by turning off 182 on Farm Road 288. Several picnic and recreational areas are located nearby.

At Alba, turn southward on Farm Road 17 to Grand Saline, home of one of the largest salt mines and plants in the country. Salt is produced from mines lying in beds extending over an area of some 30 square miles. The discovery of the salt was made by early Indian tribes. In 1845, John Jordan secured title to an acreage covering the salt deposits, blazed a trail from Nacogdoches, and hauled in two iron kettles to start a salt works here. His settlement, called Jordan's Saline, was the county seat of Van Zandt County from 1848 to 1850.

Grand Saline's salt mines were once open to visitors, but a growing number of tourists forced the operators to discontinue tours so workers would not be interrupted.

One of the principal attractions at Grand Saline is a house built of salt blocks.

Not many people know it, but Grand Saline was the home of famous aviator Wiley Post, who with Will Rogers was killed in an Alaskan air crash in 1935. Post and Harold Gatty flew around the world in a new plane, the Willie Mae, in eight days, 15 hours and 51 minutes in 1931. In 1933 Post made the trip alone in seven days, 18 hours and 49.5 minutes. Post was born near Grand Saline in 1899.

From Grand Saline, travel on Texas 110 to Van, which was established by Henry Van, an early settler. The one-time farming community had its post office at Garden Valley in Wood County until 1929 when the Jarman oil well ushered in a local oil boom. Some of the wells in the Van oil field are still pumping.

From Van, travel east on Farm Road 16 through Garden Valley and then to Lindale, where U.S. 69 will carry you back to Mineola.

During your travels, we recommend several eating places. Among them are the deli at Kitchens Hardware; and the Pineapple Tea Room, located in Sellers Corner. Both are in Mineola.

(For additional information about attractions on this Sunday Drive, contact the Mineola Chamber of Commerce, 101 East Broad Street, Mineola, Texas, 75773, telephone 214/569-2087, or the Quitman Chamber of Commerce, Box 426, Quitman, Texas 75783, telephone 214/763-4411.)

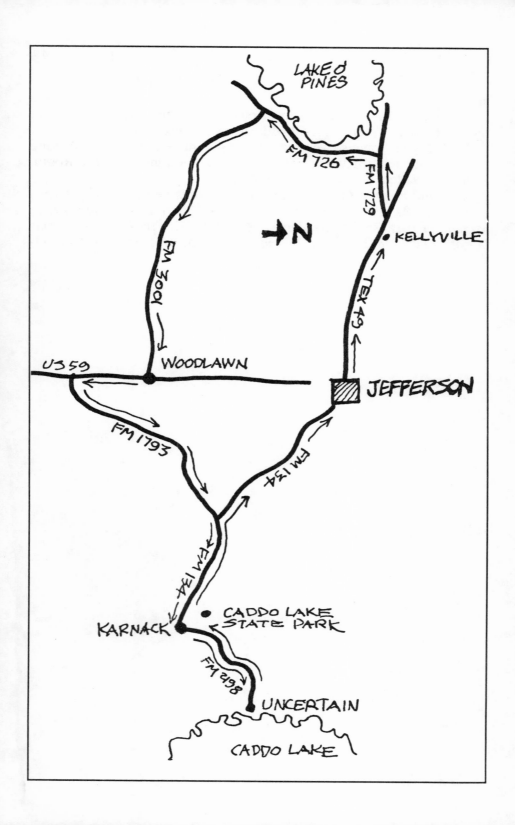

Jefferson:

Brigadoon is alive in East Texas.

Someone once called Jefferson Texas' Brigadoon, a town frozen in time, a place passed by the railroad and everything else. But Jefferson, once regarded as a dying town, thrives today as a living museum of what East Texas was all about a century ago.

This Sunday Drive takes you through Jefferson, but also skirts around some of the prettiest countryside in East Texas, an area accentuated by two interesting lakes and a lot of fascinating history.

Naturally, you should start at Jefferson. There's so much to see here, however, that you'll need help. We recommend that you pick up a historical guide at the local Chamber of Commerce. You might also want to check into the town's excellent system of Bed and Breakfast Inns if you plan to stay overnight.

You'll want to spend much of your time at Jefferson in the 20-block historical district, where historical markers are as common as mailboxes. The town, in fact, has the fifth largest number of state markers behind Austin, San Antonio, Galveston and Houston. The town also has nearly three dozen antique and souvenir stores, but they manage to avoid the cutesy and gaudy look.

It is believed that the first beer in Texas was brewed at Jefferson and that, in turn, may have led to the first commercial production of ice, also at Jefferson, in 1868.

Here are some of the main attractions of Jefferson:

• The Jefferson Museum. Formerly a post office and federal court, this handsome red-brick building houses an immense collection of items collected by the Jefferson Historical Society on three floors.

• The Excelsior House. In continuous operation since the 1850s, this magnificent old hotel has housed hundreds of dignitaries. Its luxuriously furnished rooms are filled with rare and handsomely polished antique furniture reminiscent of Jefferson in her earlier years.

• The Presbyterian Church. Built in 1872, with a specially cast bell, the church was once the largest Cumberland Presbyterian Church in Texas. The painted clock face on the steeple shows the hour for Sunday school, morning and evening worship services.

• The House of the Seasons. Noted for its interesting Victorian architecture, this Jefferson home dates back to 1872 and includes stained-glass windows, a dome with frescoes, and some historic furnishings. The house was built by Ben H. Epperson, a former Congressman.

• Jay Gould's private railroad car. Once owned by a railroad tycoon who proclaimed that Jefferson would die because it wouldn't accept his offer to run a railroad through the town, the car was restored by a local club and is now on exhibit across the street from the Excelsior Hotel.

• The Magnolias, a Greek Revival home. Built in 1867 by Dan N. Alley for his daughter, the building is unique because of its architectural details and colorful history.

There are several ways to see Jefferson without using your own car. A horse-drawn surrey and trolleys carry visitors through the downtown area and a riverboat operates on the nearby Cypress Bayou. The town also has a steam locomotive which winds past Cypress Bayou and several historic sites. During the spring, many of Jefferson's old homes—which are normally not open to the public—are opened to visitors during the Jefferson Historical Pilgrimage. Check with the local Chamber of Commerce on the dates.

We recommend several restaurants in town: The Bakery, which not only produces an excellent line of bakery goods, but some of the best Cajun-style red beans and rice in town, and Ruthmary's Restaurant, a restored Victorian residence which does an excellent job with chicken and prime rib.

If you're in town around breakfast time, make it a point to stop at the Excelsior for one of the best breakfasts in Texas. The country-cured ham and bacon, fresh eggs, grits, and orange muffins light enough to float, homemade jams and preserves, and freshly-brewed coffee—all served in a sunroom overlooking a New Orleans-style courtyard—make it an experience to cherish.

From Jefferson, continue your Sunday Drive by heading west on Texas 49. About a mile out of town, stop at the old Freeman Plantation, an antebellum home of Greek Revival style architecture with a Louisiana influence. It was constructed with pine, cypress and handmade clay bricks on a 1,000-acre cotton and sugar cane plantation in 1840. The plantation home is one of the few in East Texas open to the public on a regular basis.

As you proceed westward on Texas 49, look for a small roadside park on the right side of the highway where you'll find a state historical monument marking the site of Kellyville, a ghost town.

Long before oil shaped the state's economy, George Addison Kelly and his town were breaking ground for the coming industrialization of Texas with a simple commodity, a farmer's plow. Kellyville blossomed west of Jefferson during a time when steamboats were regularly using the waterways of Cypress Bayou. East Texas was growing, plows were in short supply, and the Kelly Plow Company supplied that need with an innovative sod-buster known as "the blue Kelly." In time, the plow became synonymous for plows among Southwestern farmers.

A few miles west of the Kellyville marker, turn left on Farm Road 729 and then make another left turn on FM 726, which will take you across the southeastern shoreline of Lake O' The Pines, sprawling over 18,700 acres. It is one of the most attractive lakes in East Texas.

FM 726 will intersect near the lake with FM 3001, which will carry you in a meandering eastern route across Marion and Harrison counties until you intersect with U.S. 59 at Woodlawn. Follow U.S. 59 south toward Marshall, but turn left on FM 1793 before you reach Marshall. When you intersect with FM 134, turn right and head toward Karnack.

Karnack, which was probably named for Karnack, Egypt, is the birthplace of Lady Bird Johnson, wife of former president Lyndon B. Johnson, a handsome two-story structure constructed of bricks made by slaves. The home was built before the Civil War and was the family home of T.J. Taylor, Mrs. Johnson's father, a well-known Karnack merchant. The home is not open to the public.

Karnack is also the home of the Longhorn Army Ammunition Plant, where Thikol Chemical Corporation produces some of the fuel used by space rockets. A few years ago, a number of U.S. missiles declared obsolete by a U.S.-Soviet peacekeeping agreement were destroyed at the site.

From Karnack, take 2198 to Caddo Lake and the town of Uncertain. Caddo Lake is made up of some 24,500 acres spreading over portions of both Texas and Louisiana. It is rich in Indian legends, including one that claims the lake was formed at night in the dark of the moon by powerful shaking spirits who were angered at a Caddo Indian chief.

There may be some factual basis for the legend. The lake was probably formed by the great New Madrid earthquake of 1811.

Steamboats from New Orleans and elsewhere regularly plied the lake in the 1800s, serving Jefferson and other settlements, and in 1869 a tragedy took 62 lives when the riverboat Mittie Stevens burned near Swanson's Landing. Jefferson residents have been trying for years to raise the 312-ton opulent riverboat or at least portions of her hull, but efforts to locate the boat have met with only limited success. Divers and nautical archaeologists have spent long hours searching the lake for the wreck, using sophisticated electronic gear.

Caddo Lake has an almost primeval aura, edged by dense cypress forests that frequently invade the waters, Spanish moss that drapes the trees, and lush aquatic growth that appears jungle-like. Because the lake's maze of channels can be confusing, the state has marked some 42 miles of boat lanes on the lake.

During the Christmas season, Uncertain—a lakeside settlement named by riverboat captains who had a hard time trying to find the port— hosts a floating Christmas parade on Caddo Lake. It is usually held on the third Sunday each December.

Before you leave the lake, be sure to visit Caddo Lake State Park, which offers excellent fishing, camping and picnicking facilities. The park is noted for its rustic cabins, which were built in 1934 by the Depression-era Civilian Conservation Corps.

From Uncertain, return to FM 134 and then to Jefferson. Before you leave the area, however, you might consider a drive 8.5 miles north of Jefferson on U.S. 59 to visit the Yellow Poplar Walking Trail. Covering a one-mile loop through land owned by International Paper Company, the trail is noted for the only stand of yellow poplar trees in Texas and, naturally, includes the state champion tree. The trail is located opposite a state roadside park.

(For more information about the places found on this Sunday Drive, contact the Jefferson Chamber of Commerce, 116 West Austin, Jefferson, TX 75657, telephone 214/665-2672.)

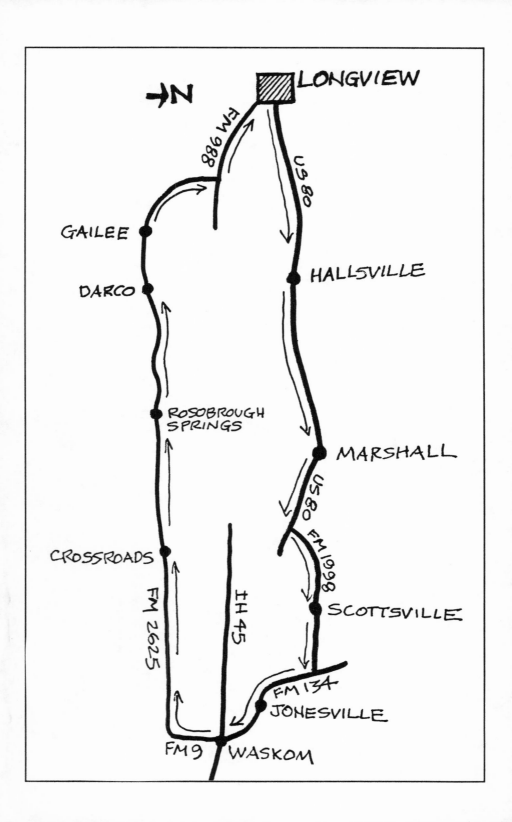

Longview & Marshall:
A metropolitan Sunday Drive.

Covering two of East Texas' principal cities, Longview and Marshall, this Sunday Drive is almost metropolitan in nature.

Begin this tour in downtown Longview with the excellent Gregg County Historical Museum at the corner of Fredonia and Bank streets. The museum's exhibits illustrate the development of Gregg County from the days of the Caddo Indians and will prepare you for the rest of your Sunday Drive.

Longview itself was carved out of the pine forests in 1870 when railroad engineers surveyed a 50-acre tract deeded to the Southern Pacific Railroad by O.H. Methvin. From the crest of Capps Hill, the surveyors, looking into the distance to the south, remarked what a "long view" there was from the hill. Longview was made the county seat of newly-created Gregg County in 1871.

Leaving the museum, you'll want to spend some time walking the streets of downtown Longview, where many of the city's oldest buildings are being preserved as the result of a strong historical movement in the community.

Be sure to see the historical marker to the last raid of the Dalton Gang at 200 North Fredonia. Here, at the First National Bank, a bloody gunfight resulted in three deaths when the Dalton Gang robbed the bank. The robbery resulted in the ultimate capture of the gang, ending its reign of crime and violence.

The Gregg County Courthouse is also in downtown Longview. Here is a statute to General John Gregg, a general in the Confederate Army.

Other Longview places of interest include:

• The Campbell Honeymoon Home, located at 521 North Second Street. This was the home of Texas Governor Thomas Mitchell Campbell when he married Fannie Bruner while working as a clerk in the Gregg County courthouse in 1878.

• The Stagecoach Stop Museum at 322 Teague, one of the few remaining homes from Earpville, the forerunner of Longview. The building dates from the early 1860s.

• The Brown-Birdsong home at 104 West Whaley Street. This Victorian home was built in 1879 by an early settler, B.W. Brown, a Methodist lay minister. Brown helped create Gregg County.

From Longview, head east on U.S. 80. You'll pass through Hallsville while traveling a scenic route characterized by meadows, ranches, and turn-of-the-century buildings. Hallsville dates back to 1839 when W.C. Crawford built a fort as protection against Indians. The town was named for pioneer Elijah Hall in 1870 when the railroad arrived.

Entering Marshall, head for the downtown area to the south of U.S. 80. In the middle of the downtown area is the Old Courthouse Museum on Peter Whetstone Square. The museum includes an excellent exhibit of everything historical in Harrison County, including Indian artifacts, pioneer relics, needlecraft, paintings and drawings, religious memorabilia, and much more.

Marshall was founded in 1842 and by 1860 was the fourth largest city in Texas. After the Civil War, it became the gateway to Texas when the Texas and Pacific Railroad provided transcontinental railway service to the west.

Marshall, named for Chief Justice John Marshall, has an abundance of historical homes and the best way to see them is to pick up a copy of Max Lale's excellent historic tour guide from the Chamber of Commerce. Most of the historic buildings are located around the downtown area and near the railroad tracks on Washington Street.

Another excellent publication is the Marshall Stagecoach Trace Guide, a driving trail of sites in Harrison County.

Some of Marshall's most interesting historical sites include:

• The Starr Family State Historic Site, known locally as "Maplecroft" for its abundance of maple trees. Located at 407 West Travis Street, the site is open Wednesday through Sunday from 9 a.m. to 4 p.m. It tells the story of a prominent East Texas family since its arrival in Texas in 1834.

• The Ginocchio Historical District on North Washington Street. The area includes the Ginocchio Hotel, once called "the finest overnight hotel and eating establishment between New Orleans and Denver." Built in the 1890s, the hotel includes a rare, curly pine staircase. Also in the historical district are several Ginocchio homes built in the 1880s, and the old Texas and Pacific Railroad Depot, one of the most interesting depots in East Texas.

• The Allen House at 610 Washington, the museum and headquarters for the Harrison County Conservation Society. The New England-style salt box house was built in 1879.

• La Maison Malfacon, located at 700 East Rusk Street, a bed-and-breakfast inn that was once the home of Texas publisher Robert W. Loughery, who became the U.S. consul to Acapulco, Mexico. The home was built in 1866.

• The site of the State Capitol of Missouri, 400 South Bolivar. The Confederate governor of Missouri moved his government-in-exile to a one-story wooden dwelling on this site during the Civil War after being run out of Missouri by federal troops.

From Marshall, head east on U.S. 80 and turn on Farm Road 1998. At the Scottsville community, take time to explore the Scottsville Cemetery, which contains some of the most elaborate statutary in East Texas. Of particular interest is a breathtaking statute of a grieving angel. The gothic revival chapel made of stone was dedicated in 1904 by Pete and Betty Scott Youree in memory of their only son, William.

Also at Scottsville is the plantation home of William Thomas Scott, who built the home in 1840 after living for several years in a log cabin.

From Scottsville, continue on 1998 until you reach the intersection of Farm Road 134. Head south on 134 to the one-time cotton community of Jonesville. Here, you'll find an honest-go-goodness general store of the kind found around the turn of the century. The T.C. Lindsey & Company General Store, which evolved from the Jones Trading Post, has been in business since 1847 and includes an enormous antique collection, as well as run-of-the mill store items. The store has been the scene of several movie and television productions. Nearby is a new museum housing rare automobiles, jukeboxes, and other memorabilia.

You'll also find at Jonesville a cotton gin, one of the last such businesses left in East Texas; the home of Dr. Samuel Floyd Vaughn, which dates back to the 1840s; and Locust Grove, a stunning two-story house with double porches built in 1847.

From Jonesville, continue on 134 to Waskom. Here, head south on Farm Road 9 until it intersects with Farm Road 2625. Follow 2625, passing through Crossroads, Rosobrough Springs, Darco and Gailee, until it reaches Farm Road 988. Head west back into Longview.

For meals, we recommend a couple of places, Johnny Cace's Seafood and Steak House, an institution in East Texas; Sally's Good Foods, also in Longview, which specializes in homestyle country meals; Gable's Restaurant in Marshall, which takes pride in its chicken, steaks and seafood entrees; and Neely's Sandwich Shop, also in Marshall, famous for its "brown pig" sandwich.

(For additional information on places found on this Sunday Drive, contact the Longview Chamber of Commerce, 100 Grand Boulevard, Longview, TX 75604, telephone 214/753-3281, or the Marshall Chamber of Commerce, P.O. Box 520, Marshall, TX 75671, telephone 214/935-7868.)

Central East Texas

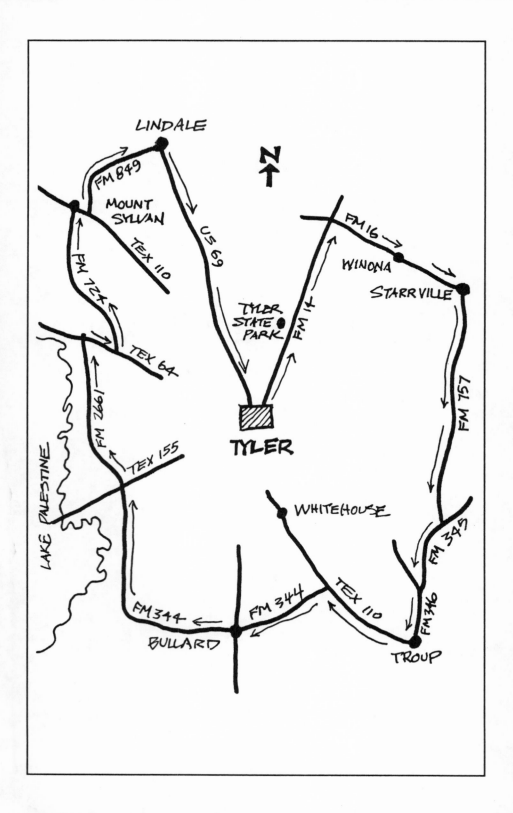

Tyler:
A drive with beauty and history.

The countryside around Tyler is both beautiful and historical, and this Sunday Drive will give you an opportunity to enjoy the two aspects at the same time.

Start your trip in downtown Tyler with a visit to the Carnegie History Center, located at 125 South College. Open Wednesday through Sunday, the Center offers an excellent overview of the history of Tyler and Smith County, starting with the days when Indians roamed the land.

You'll also want to take enough time to drive through a residential area surrounding Bergfeld Park, located on South Broadway. This area is known for its stately mansions and historic homes, many of them dating back to the 1930s when oil brought immense wealth to Tyler. Some of the streets you'll want to explore include South College, Bois d' Arc, College, Robertson and Chilton.

As you drive, pay close attention to the old brick streets. They constitute one of the largest collections of brick-surfaced streets in Texas.

Tyler, settled in the 1840s, owes its name to President John Tyler. Smith County, of which Tyler has been the only county seat, was created in 1846 from part of what is now Nacogdoches County. The county was named for General James Smith, a Texas Revolution leader who was serving in the Republic of Texas Congress when the county was named for him.

Every visit to Tyler should include a tour of the municipal Rose Gardens, the largest garden of its type in the country. Boasting over 38,000 rose bushes with more than 500 varieties, the garden is located adjacent to the East Texas Fair Grounds on West Front Street. Nearby is Rose Stadium, home of Tyler Junior College's football team.

Other attractions in Tyler include:

• The Tyler Museum of Art, located adjacent to Tyler Junior College on Mahon Street. The museum offers changing exhibits of 19th and 20th century art. It is open Tuesday through Sunday.

• Hudnall Planetarium, also on the Tyler Junior College campus. It is the only planetarium in East Texas and offers seasonal shows on a variety of celestial subjects. Call for show times and reservations.

• Brookshire's World of Wildlife, located at the Brookshire headquarters on Loop 323 in South Tyler. The museum contains more than 150 specimens of animals from across the globe with special emphasis on African and North American Wildlife. In addition, you can step back to the 1930s at an old-fashioned country store and see how grocery shopping has changed. The exhibits are open Monday through Friday.

• Caldwell Zoo, located on Martin Luther King Boulevard in North Tyler. The municipal zoo offers exhibits with more than 500 animals, making it the most complete zoo in East Texas. The zoo is open every day.

• Goodman Museum, located on North Broadway near the downtown area. This antebellum home features 19th century artifacts, antiques and period medical instruments. Days of operation change with the seasons.

• The site of Camp Ford on U.S. 271, just north of Loop 323. The Civil War prison camp housed up to 6,000 Union soldiers in the 1860s.

You may want to time your Sunday Drive with two special events, the world-famous Tyler Rose Festival, which is held in the middle of each October, and the Tyler Azalea Trail, which is held in late March and early April. Held in conjunction with the Azalea Trail is Tyler Heritage on Tour, which features several historic homes, complete with carriage rides.

When you leave Tyler, continue your Sunday Drive by heading north on Farm Road 14, which will carry you to Tyler State Park, a jewel of a recreational area carved from the pine forests. The park offers facilities for swimming, historical intrepetration, camping and picnicking.

From the Tyler State Park, continue north on 14 until the road intersections with Farm Road 16. Start south on 16 until you reach the community of Winona, which was settled in the early 1840s and named for Winona Douglas, the daughter of a prominent businessman.

At Winona, continue on 16 to the old town of Starrville, once an important overnight stop for stagecoaches and freight haulers, as well as a crucial manufacturing community. In 1869, Starrville had the Texas Fair, said by some sources to have been the first state fair in Texas.

From Starrville, turn south on Farm Road 757 until you intersect with Farm Road 345 west of Arp. Turn south on 345 until it turns into 346 and follow the latter into Troup, a one-time planters village that was developed as a railroad stop in the 1870s.

From Troup, head back toward Tyler on Texas 110, but between Troup and Whitehouse, turn east on Farm Road 344 to Bullard. Near Bullard is the old town of Burning Bush, a religious colony that existed between 1912 and 1915. The colony grew truck crops, processed fruits and tried unsuccessfully to drill for oil.

At Bullard, continue east on 344, which will carry you along the eastern edge of Lake Palestine. You can continue along the lake shoreline by picking up Farm Road 2661 at its intersection with 344 and Texas 155.

Stay on 2661 until it intersects with Texas 64. Turn to the east here on 64 until you reach the intersection with Farm Road 724. Continue in a northerly direction on 724 until you reach the Mount Sylvan community. Here, turn east on Texas 110 until you come to the intersection with Farm Road 849, which will carry you into Lindale, which dates back to 1875 when it became a stop on the railroad. Near the town is the old Steen Saline, which employed some 3,000 men during the Civil War to furnish salt for the Confederacy.

From Lindale, pick up U.S. 69 and return to Tyler.

For meals during your drive, we recommend a couple of Tyler eateries. The Hoffbrau, located on East Fifth Street not far from Tyler Junior College, serves an excellent pan-fried steak in a rustic atmosphere. Liang's, located in a shopping center at the intersection of Loop 323 and Texas 110, serves some of the finest Chinese food in East Texas.

(For additional information about places found on this Sunday Drive, contact the Tyler Area Chamber of Commerce, 407 North Broadway, Tyler, TX 75710, telephone 214/592-1661.)

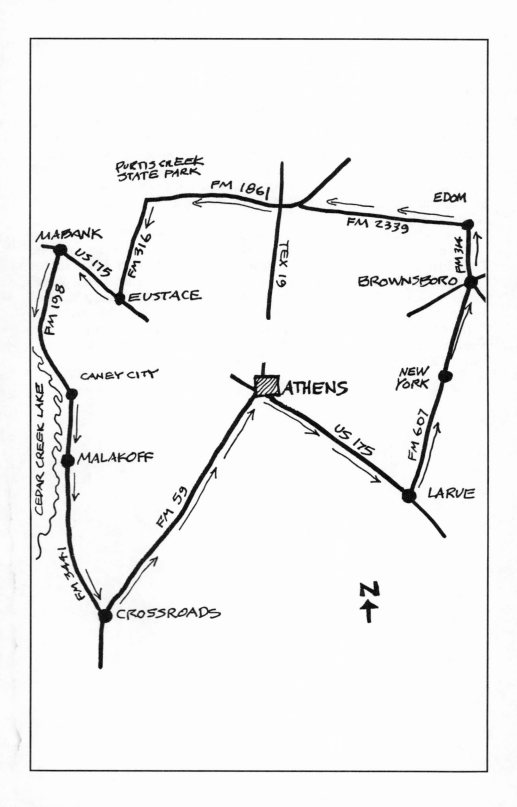

Athens:

Where the hamburger was invented.

Here's a Sunday Drive that will clear up the origin of the hamburger, carry you through a countryside that is half-East Texas and half-Central Texas, and enable you to visit several communities with interesting histories. For good measure, we've thrown in a couple of excellent Mexican food restaurants.

Start your tour in Athens, home of the hamburger and the world-famous black-eyed pea festival.

The hamburger had its beginning on Athens' interesting courthouse square in the 1880s when Fletcher Davis, who owned a downtown cafe, invented the sandwich. The delicacy was so popular that in 1904 a group of Athens businessmen raised enough money to send the inventor to the St. Louis World's Fair, where the hamburger was introduced to the world.

For many years, the growing, processing, canning and eating of black-eyed peas was a major part of life in Athens—so much so that Athens became the black-eyed pea capitol of the world, eventually spawning an annual jamboree each July.

Athens, the seat of Henderson County, was founded in 1850, four years after Texas was annexed as a state by the U.S. The county was named for J. Pickney Henderson, the first governor of Texas, and Athens was named for the Grecian capital by the step-daughter of one of the town's founders in the hope that it could become the cultural center of Henderson County.

There are a number of things to see in Athens, including:

• The B&B Cafe, established in the 1930s and named for owners Walter and Clyde Barrow. Clyde's girlfriend, Bonnie, often accompanied him to the backdoor for a meal while the sheriff, Jess Sweeten, ate in the front.

• A wealth of interesting old homes along East Tyler Street, one of the town's earliest streets. Architectural designs here range from Victorian to Colonial to Old English. The homes date back to the early 1800s.

• The Henderson County Historical Museum, housed in the 1896 Faulk-Gauntt Building. The second floor of the museum is a recreation of a turn-of-the-century law office, parlor, bedroom, bath, kitchen, and schoolroom. The museum is open to the public and is located on Prairieville Street.

• The Henderson County Courthouse, which dominates the town square.

• The Old Fiddlers Reunion, held each year in May. The festival dates back to the 1930s when the Bethel Community, near Athens, held a fiddlers contest to climax a farmer's study course. The event was moved to Athens in 1933 and is now held on the courthouse square.

From Athens, continue your Sunday Drive by heading in a southeasterly direction on U.S. 175, to the community of LaRue. The settlement was founded in 1853 when George W. Stephens built a log cabin near the present day location. The village began to develop when the New Orleans Railroad designated it as a railroad station and named it for Joe T. LaRue of Athens, who was helpful in building the railroad.

From LaRue, turn north on Farm Road 607 through the scenic countryside and stop at the settlement of New York, home of the world famous New York, Texas, Cheesecake. Everything in the bakery outlet here is wholesale priced—the cakes, the art, the crafts, even the antiques. The bakery is a wholesale bakery which sells to Neiman-Marcus, Gumpus, Horcow and other specialty stores, so the outlet is the only place where New York, Texas, Cheesecakes are sold to individuals.

From New York, continue to Brownsboro, which was settled in 1849 by John (Red) Brown, who operated a toll bridge across Kickapoo Creek on the road to Jordan's Saline and Tyler. Norwegian immigration between 1849 and 1857 brought new families into the community, and the town began to grow after building a railroad depot, a cotton gin and sawmill.

At Brownsboro, take Farm Road 314 to Edom, a small village known for its arts and crafts exhibitors. The Edom Arts Festival each year is one of the most popular rural events in East Texas. A number of artists and craftsmen from Dallas have settled in the community in recent years and produce many unusual products for metropolitan markets.

Turn west at Edom on Farm Road 2339 until you come to its intersection with Farm Road 1861, and take 1861 until it intersects with Farm Road 316 near the Purtis Creek State Park. Continuing on 316, go to Eustace, a town settled in 1874 and named for W.T. Eustace, who helped make the town a railroad stop.

From Eustace, turn north on U.S. 175 to Mabank. This town, founded about 1846 as a stop on the Texas and New Orleans Railroad, was named for two early settlers, Dodge Mason and Tom Eubanks.

At Mabank, take Texas 198, which will carry you south through several communities on the eastern side of Cedar Creek Reservoir, including Gun Barrel City, Payne Springs and Caney City. Cedar Creek lake was filled in 1964 as a water reservoir for Tarrant County, and has about 328 miles of shoreline. In 1988, the Rand McNally Retirement Places rated the lake as 14th in the nation for retirement purposes.

Follow 198 and you'll end up in Malakoff, which dates from 1850 when Dr. John Collins applied for a post office and named it for a Russian town that was prominent during the Crimean War. Silver supposedly was mined along Wild Cat Creek as early as 1830, but most of the town's latter day prosperity has come from lignite, brick clay deposits, and other resources.

At Malakoff, you should pick up Farm Road 3441, which heads south to the Cross Roads settlement. Here, take Farm Road 59 and you'll end up in Athens again.

We recommend several other eating places during the Sunday Drive: Down Mexico Way on Highway 175 west in Athens, which serves some of the best Mexican food in East Texas; Ochoa's Mexican Restaurant in Malakoff, which is equal to Down Mexico Way; the Ice House and Debe's Club at 425 North Prairieville in Athens; and the Woodshed Cafe, a downhome Edom eatery that specializes in chicken and dumplings.

(For more information about the places on this Sunday Drive, contact the Athens Chamber of Commerce, 1206 South Palestine Street, Athens, TX 75751, telephone 214/675-5181, or the Mabank Chamber of Commerce, Box 201, Mabank, TX 75147, telephone 214/887-0010.)

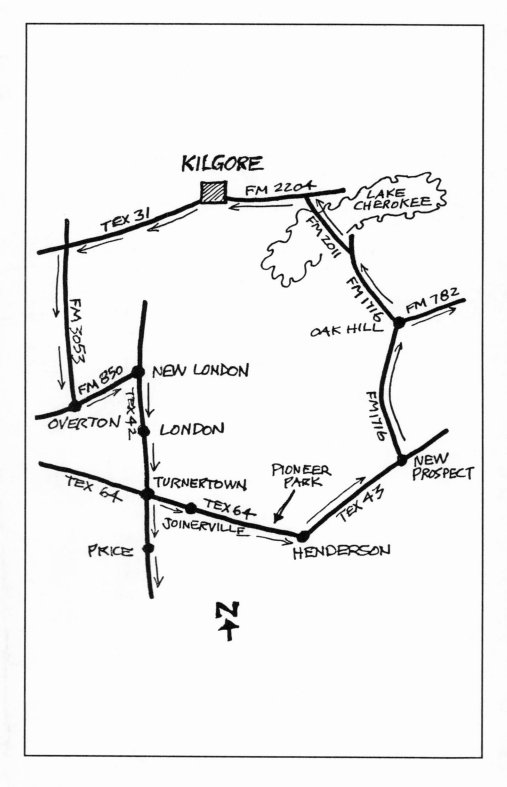

Kilgore:
What oil has wrought.

Oil put East Texas on the map in 1930 with the discovery of the East Texas Oil Field. On this Sunday Drive you'll find a number of monuments to what oil has wrought.

The biggest attraction is the East Texas Oil Museum, an excellent place to spend part of the day. Drawing attention to the museum on the campus of Kilgore College is a 72-foot wooden derrick of the kind used in the thirties, a steam boiler, rotary table and draw works. Giant wrenches serve as door handles on a doorway that opens into a world of handsome displays, photographs and memorabilia galore. Visitors can don earphones and hear recordings of the first-hand experiences of veteran drillers and children get a thrill out of taking a simulated elevator ride down 3,800 feet to the oil deposits. An excellent movie is also available in the museum.

A block behind the Museum is the Kilgore Rangerette Showcase, which pays tribute to the world's original precision dance drill team and the Kilgore College personnel who contributed to its fame. Animated props, costumes and uniforms, photographs, clippings and a Rangerettes Scrapbook are among the displays. A 10-minute film is presented in a theater.

Before leaving Kilgore, you'll want to visit the world's richest acre, a downtown lot where 24 oil derricks were drilled with their legs sitting on the same corner block. It has been estimated that the acre produced some 2.5 million barrels of crude oil selling at prices varying from $1.10 to $3.25 a barrel. In all, some 1,000 oil wells were drilled in Kilgore.

For another look at the oil industry, go to the Kilgore post office for a look at artist Xavier Gonzales' interesting Depression-era murals, "Pioneer Saga," "Drilling for Oil," "Music of the Plains" and "Contemporary Youth." The paintings were done in 1941 as part of a New Deal program to encourage embellishment of new federal buildings.

You might also want to stop at the Texan Theater, where famous horses from early western movies have their names and hoofprints imprinted in the front sidewalk.

Continue your Sunday drive at Kilgore by heading west on Texas Highway 31 toward Tyler. You'll want to stop at the Country Tavern at mealtime for some of the most famous barbecued ribs in the country. The tavern is located at the intersection of 31 and Farm Road 3053, and when you've finished with your meal, head south on 3053 toward Overton.

At Overton, veer east on Farm Road 850 to New London, where you'll find in the middle of the divided highway a large monument to one of the worst school disasters in U.S. history. On March 18, 1937, an explosion demolished the New London school, taking the lives of 293 schoolchildren and teachers. New London was established with the discovery of the East Texas Oil Field in 1930. The nearby settlement of Old London was founded around 1890, reportedly by Britishers who gave the community its name. The town, however, lost much of its identity with the founding of the newer community.

At New London, pick up Texas Highway 42, passing through Old London and Turnertown. Highway 42 will carry you through the heart of the East Texas field, where you'll see hundreds of working wells although most of them no longer have derricks. Oil companies stopped using the derricks to service the wells when they found that portable workover rigs worked just as well and were less costly to maintain.

Continue on 42 to Price. Several miles south of Price is the Jordan Plant Farm, where you'll find a wooden building fashioned in the manner of an old hotel, complete with a general store, post office, kitchen, barber shop, church, school and saloon. The central part of the building, now the general store, was once used as a hospital barracks in a movie. The Jordans bought the set, had it moved to their farm, and made additions.

After leaving the plant farm, start back up 42 until it hits the intersection with 64. Travel eastward on 64.

On 64, about seven miles west of Henderson, you'll find Pioneer Park, a park with a statute of Joe Roughneck, the symbolic hero of the oil field. The monument was erected in 1956 and includes a steel pipe containing stock to Lone Star Steel Company and other centennial papers and relics to be opened in 2056.

Not far from the park is the location of the Daisy Bradford No. 3, the well that resulted in the East Texas boom. Columbus Marion (Dad) Joiner and his geologist partner, A.D. (Doc) Lloyd, drilled the well after failing in two previous attempts to strike oil.

Continue on 64 in an easterly direction to Henderson. While in Henderson be sure to visit the best outhouse in Texas, a Victorian three-hole privy built in 1900. Standing on the grounds of the Rusk County Library, the outhouse was donated to the Rusk County Historical Commission by John and Peggy Pride and is adorned with a state historical monument. It fits in well with a group of other historical buildings that including a restored railroad depot and a log cabin.

In Henderson, don't forget to drive around Henderson's traffic circle, one of the few such traffic conveniences left in East Texas. The state's highway engineers have talked for years about replacing the circle.

Henderson is also the home of one of the country's largest gatherings of Sacred Harp singers. For more than 125 years, the East Texas contingent of singers have gathered here in August to carry on a musical legacy left by the country's early pioneers. Sacred Harp music, sometimes known as "Fa-So-La Music" or "shapenote harmony," is written with four shaped notes and sung without the accompaniment of musical instruments. The solemnization of the four shaped notes themselves serve as the prelude to the singing of the words or poetry of each song. Sacred Harp singing evolved from the melodies of England, Scotland, Ireland and Wales, brought across the Atlantic by America's first immigrants.

From Henderson, take Texas 43 toward Tatum, but leave the main highway and pick up Farm Road 1716 in the New Prospect Community. This route will carry you to Oak Hill. Take a right here on Farm Road 782 and go about four miles to the C.E. Rogers and Son General Store. Opened in 1889, the store is one of the oldest and last general stores. Washtubs still hang from the ceiling, sagging shelves hold washboards, plow handles and cow bells, and large burlaped sacks of feed still stand on the floor.

From the store, return to 1716 and then take Farm Road 2011 across Lake Cherokee and back into Kilgore via 2011 and Farm Road 2204. The route is a nice, leisurely drive through some of the prettiest rural countryside in this part of East Texas.

During your drive, we recommend several eating places in Kilgore and Henderson.

A Kilgore eatery, the Streamliner, a 1940s-style cafe, serves basic, home-cooked food and is a good place for a cup of coffee and a slice of homemade pie.

If you prefer a lighter fare, visit the oldest Dairy Queen still in business. It's just off the traffic circle in Henderson. Built in 1941, the restaurant was the second Dairy Queen opened in Texas, but the first such eatery has since gone out of business and Henderson's red-topped landmark is now in a class by itself.

(For more information about the places on this Sunday Drive, contact the Kilgore Chamber of Commerce, Box 1582, Kilgore, TX 75662, telephone 214/984-5022, or the Henderson Chamber of Commerce, Box 432, Henderson, TX 75653, telephone 214/657-5528.)

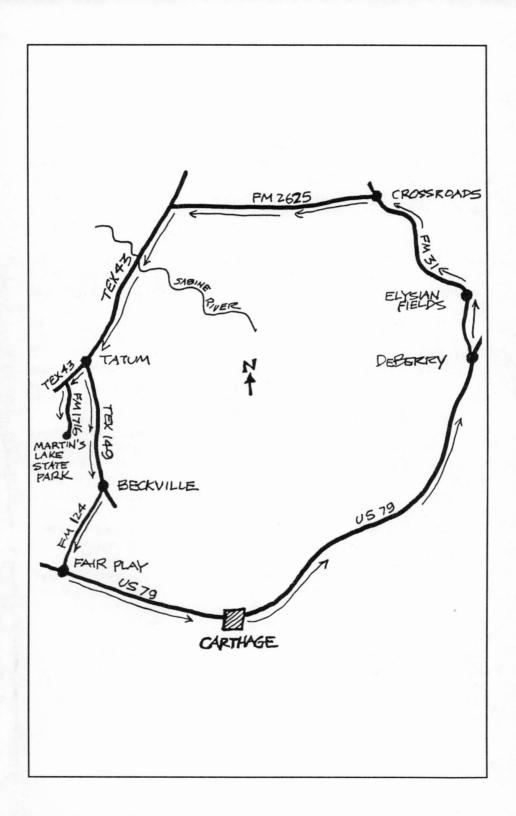

Carthage:

Music from two country masters.

Concentrated largely in Panola County, this Sunday Drive will provide you with some of the flavor of East Texas' country and western music, a look at a ghost town, a stop at an old railroad depot, and a drive through the beautiful pine and hardwood forests along the Sabine River.

Start your Sunday Drive at Carthage, the county seat of Panola County (Panola means cotton in Indian), where Potlatch, a festival of arts, crafts and country foods is held every October.

Carthage wasn't named for the foreign city, but for Carthage, Mississippi. It became the county seat in 1884 when Jonathan Allison donated 100 acres for the townsite.

If you find yourself hungry in Carthage, we recommend Joe's Cafe, which serves some of the best country-style meals in the area. The meatloaf is especially good when it's on the menu.

Joe's Cafe is located about a block off the town square, where you'll find a good collection of quaint shops as well as the Heritage Museum, located in a restored bank building, and the Panola County Historical Museum, located in the old county jail.

From Carthage, head east on U.S. 79. Four miles out of the town, on the right side of the highway, stop at the Jim Reeves Memorial, a tribute to the country singer known as "Gentleman Jim." Reeves was born near here in 1924 and grew up around DeBerry. He was killed in an airplane crash in 1964 at the peak of his career. Reeves recorded a number of successful songs, including "Bimbo," "He'll Have To Go" and "Four Walls." He also starred in a film, "Kimberly Jim."

Panola County is also the birthplace of another famous musician, Tex Ritter, who was elected to the Country Music Hall of Fame in 1964. Ritter, christened Woodward Maurice Ritter, was born here in 1907 and intended to be a lawyer. He made his first recording, "Rye Whiskey," in 1931 and became the first artist signed by Capitol Records in the 1940s. He made more than 80 western films before he died in 1974 in Nashville, Tennessee. Ritter is the father of another movie and television star, John Ritter.

At DeBerry, turn north on Farm Road 31, go through the settlement of

Elysian Fields (which means "a heavenly place"), and continue until the highway intersects with Farm Road 2625 at the crossroads. Follow it in a westerly direction until you arrive at the intersection with Texas 43. Turn south here and proceed through the town of Tatum.

Enroute you will cross the Sabine River, one of the major tributaries in East Texas. The name Sabine comes from a Spanish word meaning cypress and refers to the great growth of cypress trees found on the river's lower regions. The river, which becomes the border between Texas and Louisiana further south, was probably named by Domingo Ramon in 1716; it is so designated on a map from 1721 giving the route of the expedition led by the Marquis de Aguayo.

At Tatum, you'll find a restored Sante Fe railroad depot dating back to the days when the town bustled with railroad commerce. The depot is located in a city park about a block east of Texas 43.

Tatum was laid off in 1853 on land donated by the Tatum family when the railroad arrived.

Not far from Tatum is Hendrick's Lake, which has been attracting treasure hunters since 1913 when a man name Miller supposedly dredged up three silver bars. Treasure hunters have probed the 470-acre lake (located on private property) time and time again, using everything from ox-drawn scoops to electronic equipment. If they've found anything of value, they've kept the secret well.

The Hendrick's Lake treasure—supposedly several million in silver bars and (by some accounts) two barrels of gold nuggets—is rooted in a legend tied to freebooter Jean Lafitte, who reportedly took the loot from a Spanish ship and hired a notorious smuggler, Casper (Hot Horse) Trammel, to haul the plunder from Galveston to St. Louis over an early road known to thieves as Trammel's Trace. In what is now Panola County, Spanish calvarymen intercepted the wagon train. In desperation, Trammel ordered the wagons pushed into Hendrick's Lake and fled with his men.

When you leave Tatum, drive a few miles south of the community on Texas 43 and take a left on Farm Road 1716. You'll come to a dead end at historic Harmony Hill Cemetery, one of the last vestiges of the old town of Harmony Hill, once a trading settlement. Just down the road from the cemetery is Martin's Lake State Park, a small but attractive lake overlooked by an electrical generating plant. Harmony Hill was a prosperous trading center on Trammell's Trace, but died when the railroad came to Tatum, bypassing merchants on the old road.

Back on Texas 43, return to Tatum, take Texas 149 southeast to the settlement of Beckville, which was founded before the 1880s by Matthew W. Beck, who settled in the area about 1850. The town was originally established about a mile north of its present site but was moved in 1887 to be near the railroad.

At Beckville, take FM 124 and proceed in a southerly direction until you come to the community of Fair Play at the intersection with U.S. 79. Travelers supposedly gave the town its name in gratitude for the way they were treated at John Allison's store, hotel and blacksmith shop in the 1850s. One legend tells the story of a young girl, member of a wagon train moving west, who died here and was buried in a local cemetery. Over the years, townspeople have tended to the grave as if it were one of their own.

Just down the road from Fair Play is another rural village known as Rake Pocket, which supposedly got its name because merchants often cheated visitors.

From Fair Play, take U.S. 79 back to Carthage, completing your Sunday Drive.

(For more information about the places found on this Sunday Drive, contact the Carthage Chamber of Commerce, 316 West Panola Street, Box 207, Carthage, TX 75633, telephone 214/693-6634.)

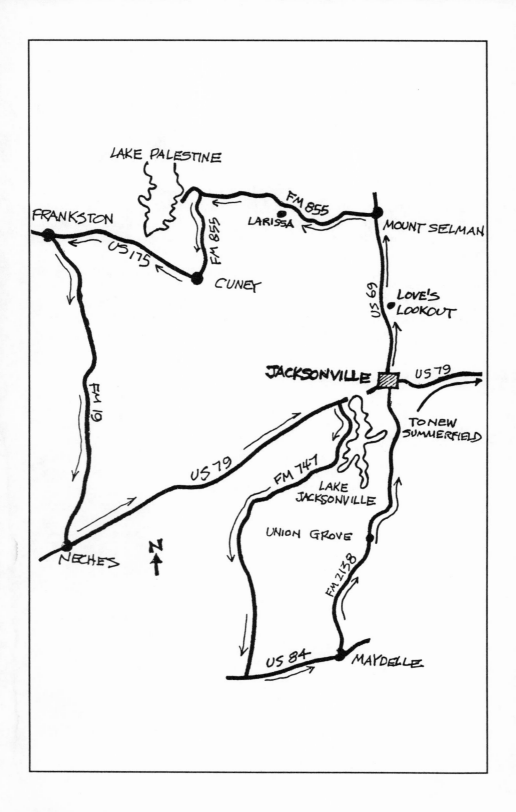

Jacksonville:

Indians, bargains, and chicken fried steaks.

Beginning at Jacksonville, here's a Sunday Drive with a hefty dose of Indian history, several stops that offer bargains in factory goods and springtime plants, a long stretch of magnificent rural countryside, and a popular chicken fried steak.

With several large factory outlets, Jacksonville offers some excellent bargains for shoppers. Just north of the city, on the right side of U.S. 69, is the Lobby Shop of a lingerie company, which is open from 9 a.m. to 5 p.m. Monday through Saturday and Sunday from 1 to 5 p.m. Another lobby shop at the Texas Basket Factory is also open seven days a week. The East Texas Handbag Company offers bargains on the first Saturday of each month and the Jacksonville Candy Company has an outlet open five days a week.

The candy company makes a unique candy bar that consists largely of crushed peanuts, corn syrup, sugar, salt and milk. The bar, sold throughout East Texas, is known as Holcomb's Special Bar, but East Texans have labeled it as "The Greasy Bar" because of its oily appearance and taste.

While you're in Jacksonville, stop at the Vanishing Texana Museum, a part of the city's public library, and you might want to visit the Old City Cemetery, where the famous blind whistler, Fred Lowery, is buried. Lowery's rendition of "The High and The Mighty" for the John Wayne movie sold 1.7 million records. Lowery started his career with WFAA Radio in Dallas and later performed with the Horace Heidt Orchestra during the Big Band era. He was a resident of Jacksonville but was born in Palestine.

If you have time, drive by the Tomato Bowl, one of the oldest high school football stadiums in East Texas; it is unusual because the iron-ore rocks used in its construction were quarried in Cherokee County.

If hunger strikes you in Jacksonville, there are a couple of interesting eating places—Stacy's Barbecue, which serves consistently good barbecue from a remodeled home on U.S. 69 south, and Jacksonville Station, which does a good job with chicken, steaks and seafood.

For a delightful side trip, especially during the spring, drive a few miles east of Jacksonville on U.S. 79 to New Summerfield, where you'll find excellent bargains in plants, flowers, hanging baskets and other greenery. New Summerfield has one of the largest collections of greenhouses and plant farms in Texas, and many of the growers operate roadside shops catering to springtime motorists. It's an excellent place to buy hanging baskets which sell here for $5 to $10, compared with $10 and $20 elsewhere.

When you return to Jacksonville, drive north on U.S. 69 five miles until you reach Love's Lookout Park with one of the most breathtaking views in East Texas. The park, named for pioneer orchard owner John Wesley Love, sits on a nine-mile long ridge with several lookout points which command a view of 30 to 35 miles. At Love's Lookout is one of the last fire lookout towers left over from the days when state forest fire fighters scaled the structures to seek out smoke signs. The fire fighters use planes today and the old towers are slowly vanishing from the forests.

Between the two lookout points of Love's Lookout and Mount Selman is a narrow valley known as McKee's Gap for Thomas McKee, who led a group of Presbyterians here from Tennessee and began the town of Larissa.

Larissa is today a ghost town and you'll find its ruins—a few rotting buildings and a state historical marker—by travelling north on U.S. 69 and then turning west on FM 855 at Mount Selman. Local legend says the first matched game of baseball in Texas was played here.

Near Larissa is the site of the Killough Massacre, where 18 members of the Killough, Wood and Williams families were killed or carried off by Indian raiders in 1838. Bodies of the few victims who were found were buried in a small cemetery deep in the woods. The site is worth visiting, but we recommend that you ask a local resident for directions; the roads are unmarked and difficult to find.

Continue on FM 855 and you'll find yourself at the edge of Lake Palestine, a 25,560-acre lake popular with fishermen, boaters and campers.

FM 855 will also carry you to the community of Cuney, where you should turn west to Frankston on U.S. 175. Hhere you'll find an interesting landmark, the town's restored railroad depot. And not far from the town is Dabb's Cemetery, where legend says a man was buried alive (relatives incorrectly thought he was dead), dug his way out of the graveyard, and crawled to a nearby home and died. When he was buried a second time, local residents supposedly put a fence of wooden stakes around the grave to make sure he wouldn't crawl out again.

Another Frankston cemetery, Brush Creek, contains the grave of Cynthia Ann Parker, who was kidnapped by Commanche Indians at the age of nine, lived with the Indians for 35 years and married Chief Pete

Nacona. Cynthia Ann and her baby daughter, Prairie Flower, were recaptured by whites in 1860 but never adjusted to life among the whites and died following the death of her baby daughter. One of Cynthia's sons by Chief Nacona was Quanah Parker, leader of the Commanches in their final stand against the whites in 1875.

While you're in Frankston, visit Ellis Mercantile, an honest-to-goodness general store with everything from seed to hardware.

At Frankston, pick up FM 19 and at this point, you'll begin one of the most scenic rural drives in East Texas. Follow FM 19 South to Neches, then travel on U.S. 79 back toward Jacksonville until you reach the intersection of FM 747 (you'll want the southern intersection heading to Lake Jacksonville). Follow 747 along the lake, through the settlement of Pierce's Chapel, and then to the I.D. Fairchild State Forest.

Named for State Senator I.D. Fairchild of Lufkin, the state forest covers some 2,740 acres in five tracts. The forest was originally owned by the state prison at nearby Rusk and includes one small day-use area with fishing, hiking and picnicking facilities about a quarter mile south of U.S. 84.

Take U.S. 84 to the town of Maydelle, and you'll find the rustic Maydelle Cafe, home of one of the best chicken-fried steaks in East Texas. Maydelle is also one of the stops on the route of the Texas State Railroad, which operates steam passenger excursion trains between Rusk and Palestine. Maydelle was named in a circuitous manner for Gov. Tom Campbell's daughter. The daughter's name was Mabelle, but the town's founders discovered there existed a town bearing the name, so they settled for Maydelle by changing one letter.

Turn north at Maydelle on FM 2138 through the Union Grove community and then back to Jacksonville.

(For more information about the places found on this Sunday Drive, contact the Jacksonville Chamber of Commerce, 506 S. Rusk, Box 1231, Jacksonville, TX 75766, telephone 214/586-2217.)

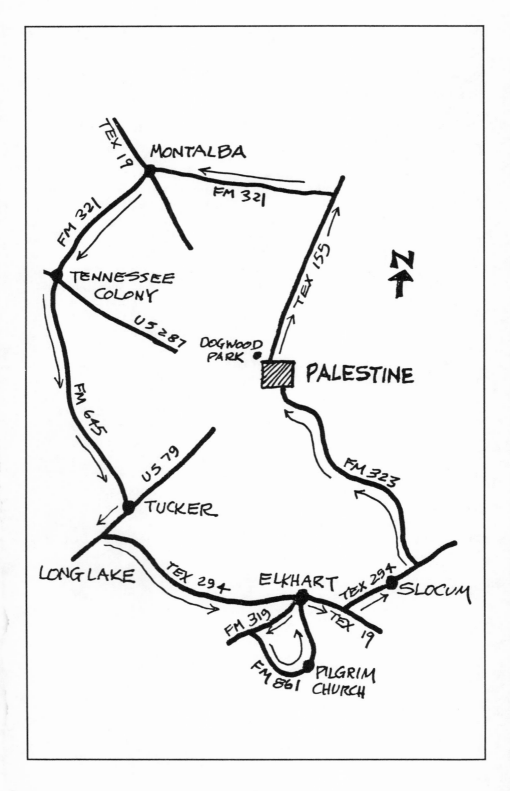

Palestine:

Old homes, fruit cakes, and stained glass windows.

The focal point of this Sunday Drive is Palestine, the county seat of Anderson County and a town whose history parallels the arrival of the railroad in the 1870s. But you'll also have the opportunity to see some excellent rural scenery.

Start your Sunday Drive with a tour of downtown Palestine. The Chamber of Commerce offers an excellent walking tour guide which will carry you to several points of interest, including:

• The Redlands Hotel at 400 North Queen. Now a nostalgic galleria of specialty shops, the old hotel thrived from 1915 to 1918 and then served as an office building for the next four decades.

• Carnegie Public Library, located at 502 North Queen. Built in 1915, the building is a recorded Texas historical landmark.

• Kolstad's Jewelers, located at the corner of Oak and Sycamore. This business is known as the oldest continuous retail store in Texas and the oldest jewelry store west of the Mississippi River.

• Eilenberger's Bakery, located at 500 North John, known for its world-famous fruit and pecan cakes. The bakery has been in business since 1898.

• The Museum of East Texas Culture, originally the old Palestine High School. Exhibits in the museum deal with various aspects of Anderson County's history, including an excellent section on railroad history. The museum is located adjacent to the John H. Reagan Monument and Park near the downtown area.

Palestine also offers a wealth of Victorian homes, located primarily on Sycamore, Perry, Hodges, Link, Kolstad, Mallard, Magnolia, Reagan and Royall streets. Few of the homes, however, are open to the public, but that shouldn't stop you from enjoying the exteriors during a drive-by.

Another feature of Palestine is its abundance of stained glass church windows, including those at Sacred Heart Catholic Church, 503 North Queen; First Christian Church, 113 East Crawford; the First Presbyterian Church, 410 Avenue A; First United Methodist Church, 422 South

Magnolia; St. Philips Episcopal Church, 106 East Crawford; and Grace United Methodist Church, located at Kolstad and Queen.

Palestine is also the western terminal of the Texas State Railroad, which runs regular passenger service with old steam locomotives and restored coaches between the city and Rusk. The tours start around Memorial Day and end around Labor Day. Be sure to check with the local Chamber of Commerce for reservation information.

Five miles west of Palestine on Texas 287 is the National Scientific Balloon Facility, the launching site for balloons reaching high altitudes. Visitors are welcome, but you should call ahead for reservations.

To continue your Sunday Drive beyond Palestine, turn north on Texas 155, but before you leave the city limits, turn to the left on Link Road and make a drive through Davey Dogwood Park, a spectacular area during the spring when the dogwoods are in bloom. The park's main road winds five miles through the 400-acre park.

Return to 155 and continue north to its intersection with Farm Road 321. Near the intersection is a state historical marker noting the importance of two Anderson County towns, Plenitude and Mound Prairie, during the Civil War. Both settlements, now ghost towns, made rifles, grist mills and cotton gins used in the Confederate war effort.

At the highway intersection, turn east toward Montalba community, which lies at the intersection of 321 and Texas 19. The town's distinctive name comes from a nearby mountain.

From Montalba, continue in a western direction on 321 to Tennessee Colony.

From Tennessee Colony, head south on Farm Road 645 to Tucker, named for an early settler known as Colonel Tucker.

Near Tucker, on U.S. 79, you'll find Old Magnolia, a cluster of old buildings representing turn-of-the-century life in East Texas. The theme park, built by schoolteacher/carpenter Bill Gibbs, is open during the Dogwood Trails season and for special events such as group gatherings.

Continue in a westerly direction to Long Lake, where you should veer back to the east on Texas 294 toward Elkhart. A few miles from the intersection, look for a historical marker to Old Magnolia, a Trinity River steamboat port. In the 1850s, Magnolia consisted of about 800 residents and included a drug store, land office, blacksmith shop, tavern, cotton gin, general store, school, church and a hotel, the Hagood, known all over Texas for its hospitality. Dozens of steamboats docked at the town's wharves, but the railroad eventually killed trade on the river.

Continue your Sunday drive to Elkhart, named for a friendly Indian who helped early settlers. At Elkhart, head west on Farm Road 319, and then turn south on Farm Road 861 to the Pilgrim Church and Cemetery, which has been in continuous use since 1833 when Rev. Daniel Parker built a small log house of worship. A replica of his original church still stands on the site. The Parker family earned an additional place in Texas history when a Comanche war party attacked Parker Fort near Mexia, kidnapping Cynthia Ann Parker, who adopted the ways of the Indians and married Comanche chief Pete Nacona.

When you leave Pilgrim, continue on 861, which will carry you back to Elkhart. Then turn south on Texas 19, but pick up Texas 294 to Slocum a few miles out of Elkhart. Continue through Slocum until you come to the intersection with Farm Road 323, which will return you to Palestine. Slocum enjoys one of the oddest names in East Texas; it was named by a local wit because of the slowness in securing a post office which was finally established in 1898. "It's been slow to come," he reportedly remarked.

For meals, we recommend Lobo's Little Mexico at Palestine, one of the best Mexican food restaurants in East Texas,

(For additional information about places found on this Sunday Drive, contact the Palestine Visitor and Convention Bureau, P.O. Drawer I, Palestine, TX 75801, telephone 214/723-3014.)

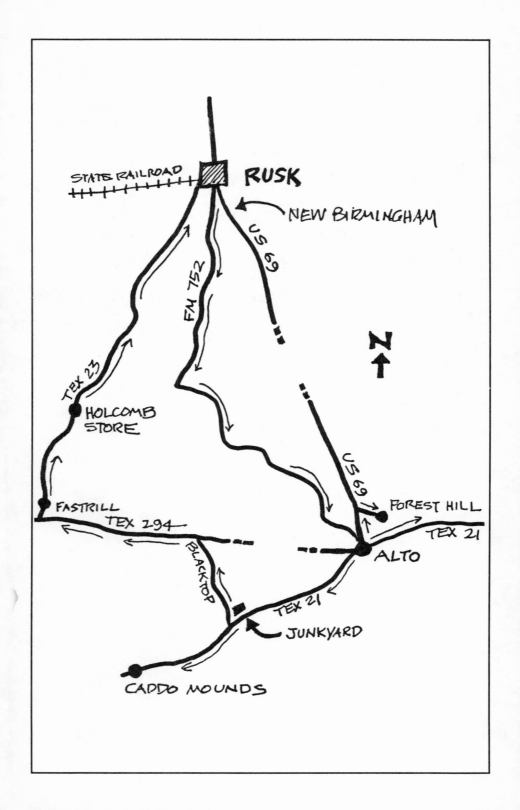

Rusk:

Mark Twain might have lived here.

This Sunday Drive will find you in the pine-clad hills of Cherokee County and the town of Rusk, which is one of those places where you wish you had spent your youth. Its tree-lined streets, busy courthouse square, and stately turn-of-the-century buildings are the stuff Mark Twain wrote about.

To start your Sunday Drive, first spend some time in Rusk, which was named for Thomas J. Rusk, a Texas revolutionary war hero whose name has been borrowed by the Thomas J. Rusk Hotel, located on the town square. It's a good place to start a walking tour of Rusk.

Your tour should include the Rusk Post Office, where you'll find a mural painted by Bernard Beruch Zakheim, an immigrant from Poland who studied under Diego Rivera. Zakheim's mural was painted in 1939 as part of a federal program to provide work for qualified artists and to embellish federal buildings.

Your tour should also include the J.W. Summers home, built in 1884 and one of Rusk's most attractive old homes; the Perkins home, with its distinctive gabled wood carving featuring a star and rising sun; and the Confederate soldier on the courthouse square, which is unique because it faces south instead of north as most Confederate statues do.

Rusk has a history of involvement in the Civil War and you'll find a number of interesting historical sites around the city, including a Confederate gun factory site on U.S. 84 west of the city and a Union prisoner-of-war compound two miles south of the city on FM 241, where some 3,000 Union prisoners were housed. The town was also a Confederate manufacturing center, producing wagons, saddles, harnesses, guns, plows, skillets and other items.

Before you leave the downtown area, be sure to walk the Rusk Footbridge, which is believed to be the longest in the nation—some 546 feet long. During its early years, before streets connected a residential area with the downtown business district, the bridge served as a means to cross a small valley when the creek flooded. The bridge was built by Howard

Barnes, an engineer who also designed the nearby ghost town of New Birmingham.

You'll find what's left of New Birmingham a few miles south of downtown Rusk on U.S. 69. A large granite monument stands in front of the Texas Highway Department on the east side of the highway and, less than a mile south, look for a small walking trail on the west side of the highway. The trail weaves its way around an old iron furnace site.

The furnace was one of several which propped up the New Birmingham economy in the 1890s when the town was being heralded as one of the most promising cities in Texas. However, the economic panic of 1893, coupled with an explosion at one of the furnaces, killed the town.

Back in Rusk, one of the state's smallest bank buildings, the old Bonner Bank, stands near the New Southern Hotel on U.S. 69. It was operated as Cherokee County's first bank between 1884 and 1892 by F.W. Bonner.

Rusk is also the home of the Texas State Railroad and the site of Jim Hogg State Park. Located just off U.S. 84 east of Rusk, the park pays tribute to the first native-born governor of Texas. Hogg was one of two Texas governors born in Rusk; the other was Thomas M. Campbell.

The 177-acre Hogg park, originally the home of the governor, was once called "Mountain Home" and rests on a mountain about 200 feet above the rest of Rusk. Even on the hottest days, park visitors will find a soothing breeze in the park. A replica of Hogg's old home is used as a museum.

Gov. Campbell's birthplace is four miles northeast of Rusk on FM 768, off U.S. 69, but only a state historical marker is left on the spot.

In Rusk, you'll also find the Rusk State Hospital, which was built originally as a state prison in 1877-79. Some of the prison's old buildings still stand on the grounds.

From Rusk, take Farm Road 752, which will carry you south through the gently rolling hills of Cherokee County toward Alto. Hulen Wilcox's syrup mill is located just off the farm road, but he only operates the mill during the late fall when his cane crop is ready. When the mill is working, Hulen usually puts a sign on the side of FM 752.

Follow 752 into Alto. There are several theories about the origin of the town's name. An early pioneer is supposed to have suggested the name because he felt that Alto was the Latin word for high. Another story says the name was chosen because Alto is the Spanish word for stop.

There are several sites near Alto worth side trips. A few miles east on Texas Highway 21, you'll find a miniature park and gravesite of Helena Kimble Dill Nelson, mother of the first child believed to have been born to Anglo-Americans in Texas. Five miles northeast of Alto on the Rusk-Linwood Road is Forest Hill, the one-time plantation home of Captain James Berryman and his wife, Helena Dill Berryman, that historic first child. Forest Hill is open to the public during the second and third weekends in October.

When you return to Alto from the two side trips, start in a southwesterly direction on Texas Highway 21 and travel about six miles to the Caddo Mounds State Historic Site.

Here you'll find evidence of Indians who lived in East Texas thousands of years ago. The early Caddos lived on the site around 800 A.D. The alluvial prairie near the Neches River had ideal qualities for the establishment of a village and ceremonial center, good sandy loam soil for agriculture, abundant natural food resources in the forest, and a permanent water source in the nearby river. The historical site includes an excellent museum and interpretation center, a replica of a Caddo structure, and ceremonial mounds.

After leaving the Caddo site, return to Texas 21 and start back toward Alto, but a few miles up the road, take a left turn by a junkyard (which is a good place to browse for offbeat items and antiques) and Thomas Chapel church. You'll be on a blacktop country road which will take you past scenic farmhomes, spring-fed creeks and open pastures. The country lane is especially scenic during the spring and fall. Follow the road until you reach its intersection with Texas 294, take a left and start westward.

Just before you reach the Neches River, turn north on Texas 23 by a roadside park. Not far from the roadside park is the Arthur Temple Sr. Research Center, an area maintained by the Texas Forest Service. The Center sits on land once occupied by Fastrill, a ghost town operated by Southern Pine Lumber Company as a logging camp in the 1940s.

Texas 23 will take you through another stretch of rolling hills, past the communities of Holcomb's Store and Beulah, and back into Rusk.

We recommend a couple of good eating places on this Sunday Drive. Dot's Cafe, a black-owned cafe on Martin Luther King Street in Rusk, serves some of the best soulfood in East Texas, but Dorothy Jackson only serves luncheon meals. Ask Dorothy for a sampling of her special hot relish—a recipe she keeps closely guarded. Also in Rusk, the dining room of the Thomas J. Rusk Hotel serves several excellent dishes, including good steaks, a nice Cornish hen, and an excellent bread pudding.

If you like to cook, we recommend the Foot Bridge Garden Cookbook, which was organized and published by the Cherokee County Heritage Association. The cookbook contains recipes for such dishes as Pepper Jelly, Baked Black Eyed Peas, Cracklin' Bread and Old Fashioned Biscuits. Many of the recipes date back to the 1800s. For a copy, write Foot Bridge Garden Cookbook, P.O. Box 590, Rusk, Texas 75785.

(For more information about the places found on this Sunday Drive, contact the Rusk Chamber of Commerce, Box 67, Rusk, TX 75785, telephone 214/683-4242, or the Alto Chamber of Commerce, Box 536, Alto, TX 75925, telephone 409/858-4713.)

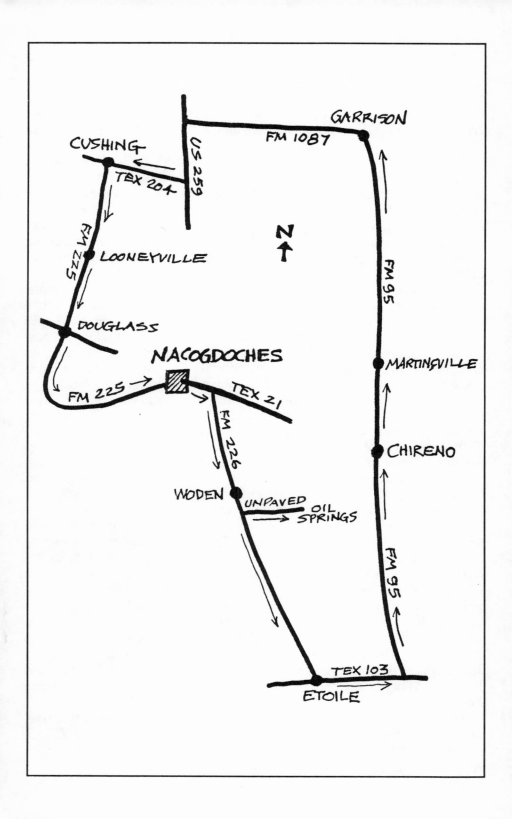

Nacogdoches:
Start with the Alamo of East Texas.

Nacogdoches is so resplendent in history that it's difficult to develop a Sunday Drive that takes you out of its city limits.

So we advise you to spend some time in the town that calls itself Texas' oldest city, starting with the Stone Fort, a building affectionately called "the Alamo of East Texas."

The histories of the two forts are vastly different, but the Stone Fort, built in 1779 as a Spanish trading post, does offer a good overview of what early East Texas was like. It sits on the campus of Stephen F. Austin State University and before you leave the campus, you might want to look over a nearby monument to Lyne Taliaferro (Tol) Barret, who is credited with drilling Texas' first oil well (more about this later).

Hitting all of Nacogdoches' historic sites can take a week, so here are some of the highlights:

• Millard's Crossing. Located on North Street, this superb collection of early East Texas buildings—including everything from a barber shop to a church—is the only town of its kind in Texas. It was started by Mrs. Lera Thomas, wife of Houston Congressman Albert Thomas. She lives on the grounds.

• The Sterne-Hoya Home in downtown Nacogdoches, where Sam Houston was baptized into the Catholic religion in order to own land in Texas.

• Oak Grove Cemetery, burial place of four signers of the Texas Declaration of Independence and including some of the most interesting stonework in East Texas. One tombstone, resembling the San Jacinto Monument, looms above the grave of Thomas J. Rusk, first secretary of war for the Republic of Texas, one of Sam Houston's commanders at San Jacinto, and a State Senator. He was buried here in 1857, a tragic suicide victim.

• The Old Nacogdoches University Building, the only structure still standing from a non-sectarian university chartered under the Republic of Texas. It is now a museum.

• Old North Church, believed to be the oldest union church in Texas.

Several denominations worshipped here, including the Baptists who gathered under a large oak tree on the site in 1835.

• Antique shops—lots of them. At last count, there were 23 in Nacogdoches.

When you've finished touring Nacogdoches, start your Sunday Drive by heading east on Texas Highway 21, sometimes called El Camino Real, the Old San Antonio Highway, or the King's Highway. Whatever you call it, the route has been in existence since 1691 when Spanish missionaries first used it to establish outposts in frontier Texas. Today's highway is much easier to travel and the scenery—punctuated by verdant forests and gently rolling hills—deserves a leisurely pace.

A few miles out of Nacogdoches, turn south on Farm Road 226 toward Woden. Continue through the community until you come to a sign pointing the way via an unpaved logging road to Oil Springs, a ghost town where Tol Barret drilled his pioneer oil well in 1866.

Although Barret went broke in trying to develop an oil field, a number of other wells were drilled in the area in the 1870s and around the turn of the century, leading to the creation of a rough-hewn village in the woods. There's not much left at Oil Springs today except a few old storage tanks, some oily springs, and a few rusty, shallow wells. The forests around Oil Springs are magnificent any time of the year.

Return to Farm Road 226 and proceed south until you reach Etoile. Turn east on Texas 103 until you reach the intersection with Farm Road 95. Turn north to the settlement of Chireno, where you'll find some of the prettiest Victorian-style homes in East Texas. Of particular interest is the town's famous Gingerbread Home. Chireno, named for the Jose Antonio Chireno land grant, dates back to 1837 when it was founded by Dr. J.N. Fall. Not far from town is the Halfway House, a one-time stagecoach stop on the El Camino Real; the landmark is in the process of being restored.

At Chireno, continue on 95 to Martinsville. Just west of Martinsville on Texas 7 in the Swift community is one of the most scenic areas in Deep East Texas, the Carl Monk Overlook, which offers an excellent view of the timbered bottomlands of the Attoyac River.

At Martinsville—once known as Martin City for Dr. John D. Martin, who opened the first business here in 1857—continue on 95 until you arrive in Garrison. Named for Frank Garrison, the town dates back to 1882 when it was established as a stop on the Houston, East and West Texas Railroad.

From Garrison, follow Farm Road 1087 westward until it intersects with U.S. 259. Drive south a few miles and turn in a westward direction on Texas 204 until you reach Cushing, a town that was organized in 1903 with the coming of the Texas and New Orleans Railroad and named for Edward B. Cushing, chief engineer of the railroad.

At Cushing, pick up Farm Road 225 and enroute you'll pass through the community of Looneyville, a rural crossroads settlement where college kids from Nacogdoches keep stealing the town signs. Stop at the Looneyville General Store for a visit with the porchsitters and then follow 225 into Douglass. This settlement was laid out in 1836 by Michael Costly on an 800-acre tract of land he bought from John Durst. Named for Kelsey H. Douglass, the town was the site of a stagecoach inn on the Old San Antonio Road.

From Douglass, continue on 225 and it will return you to Nacogdoches. You may want to stop at Lake Nacogdoches, a peaceful little reservoir tucked away in the pineywoods. You'll find a number of lakeside picnic areas where you can stop and enjoy the sights.

For meals, we recommend several places where the food is good and fairly inexpensive:

• The Cotton Patch on North Street, which specializes in down-home country cooking (the meatloaf is exceptional).

• La Hacienda, also on North Street, a beautifully-restored, 1913-era lumberman's home that doubles as a Mexican food restaurant (we liked the seafood enchiladas).

• Casa Tomas, another good Mexican restaurant, about a block from La Hacienda on the opposite side of North Street.

(For more information about the places found on this Sunday Drive, contact the Nacogdoches Chamber of Commerce, 1801 North Street, Box 1918, Nacogdoches, TX 75963, telephone 409/564-7351.)

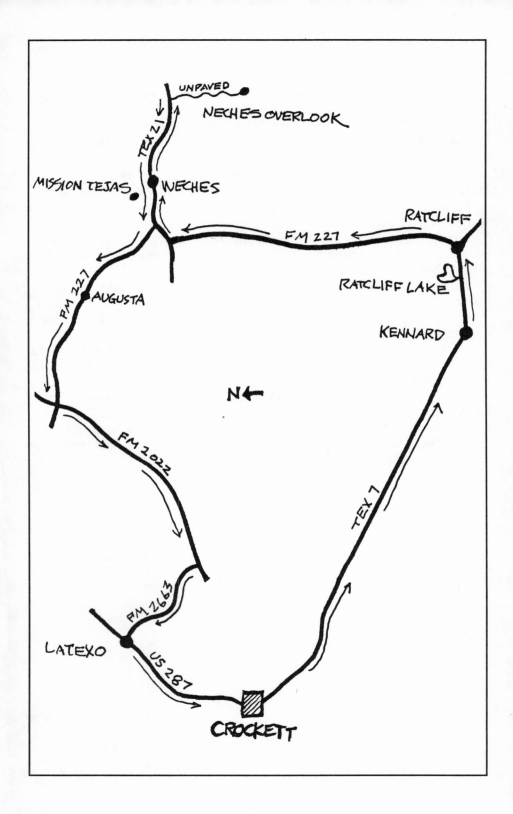

UNPAVED

NECHES OVERLOOK

TEX 21

MISSION TEJAS   WECHES

RATCLIFF

FM 227

RATCLIFF LAKE

FM 227   AUGUSTA

KENNARD

N←

FM 2022

TEX 7

FM 2663

LATEXO

US 287

CROCKETT

Crockett:

Houston County, not Houston, Texas.

This Sunday drive is all packed within a single county, Houston County, not to be confused with Harris County, which is the home of Houston.

Houston County was the first Texas county incorporated in the state, dating back to 1836. Our starting point, the city of Crockett and the county seat of Houston County, claims to be the fifth oldest in the state.

One of the biggest attractions in Crockett is its abundance of restored historical homes, many of them located along Houston Street (Texas Hwy. 21), once the major entry point to the city.

Among the city's best-known homes are the Monroe-Crook house (709 Houston), built in 1854 by A.T.M. Monroe, a great-nephew of President James Monroe; the Robert Emmett McConnall house (617 East Houston), built in 1901; the Edmiston-Driskell home (902 East Houston), a large antebellum-style residence constructed in 1904 by C.L. Edmiston; the Dan McLean home (1105 East Houston), built in the 1890s by Dan McLean, grandson of the first permanent settler of Houston County; the Castleberg residence (721 East Houston), a Greek Revival structure built sometime before 1887 by H.C. Castleberg; the Denny-Larson home (1102 East Houston), which dates back to 1907; the Moore-LeGory-Denny residence (923 East Houston), built around 1895 by Harry Fred Moore, president of a local bank; the Elliott Stokes residence, dating back to 1912; the Arledge home (718 East Houston), built in the 1890s by the Goolsby family and later expanded by the Arledges; the S.C. Arledge home (900 East Houston), built around 1892; and the Elliott Stokes home (922 East Houston), which dates back to 1912.

Two Houston Street churches—the All Saints Episcopal Church at 1301 East Houston and the First Presbyterian Church at 713 East Houston—are also worth visiting because of their rich history.

Some other Crockett structures worth mentioning include the A.E. Gossett house, built around 1838 near El Camino Real (Texas 21) by Andrew Edwards Gossett, whose father Elijah was a Tennessee neighbor of Davy Crockett and who gave Crockett its name; the Downes-Aldrich house (207 North Seventh) a magnificent Victorian mansion constructed in the early 1890s by J.E. Downes, a local merchant; and the Strode-Pritchell log cabin, located in Davy Crockett Memorial Park. The cabin was built either or by both William W. Wallace or Benjamin Wallace around 1843 on a land grant about 12 miles east of Crockett.

Another building worth a visit is the Crockett Railroad Depot at 303 South First. County historians are trying to restore the depot as a visitors center for the community.

If you become hungry in Crockett, we suggest a couple of stops—the Wooden Nickle, a rustic restaurant worth visiting because of its excellent hamburgers and proliferation of wall signs and antiques; the Crockett Inn, best-known for its homemade breads; and the King's Inn. All are located on Loop 304 on the east side of town.

Before leaving Crockett, be sure to visit Davy Crockett's spring, where the Alamo defender supposedly camped on his way to San Antonio. The spring is located off the Crockett town square near a railroad underpass.

From Crockett, head east on Texas Highway 7, which will carry you into the heart of the Davy Crockett National Forest and some of the most diverse timberlands in East Texas. Between Lufkin and Crockett visitors will find magnificent stands of mature pines century-old bottomland hardwoods, acres of young pines, and everything else you'd expect to find in the pineywoods. At the same time, virtually every kind of forest management practice—from clearcutting to selective cutting—is found along the roadside. Most of the forests here are managed by the U.S. Forest Service and several large forest product companies.

As you travel, look for the black aluminum historical markers along the highway, including several marking the sites of ghost towns.

Between the towns of Kennard and Ratcliff, take a left turn into the Ratcliff Lake Recreational Area, an excellent picnicking, camping and fishing area. At the Concession Stand near the lake, pick up a copy of an audio tour tape that will carry you on a guided trip around the recreational areas, as well as through other parts of the Davy Crockett National Forest. The tour takes about an hour and a half, but it is well worth the drive. Most of the roads you will travel during the tour will be unpaved.

Just east of the Recreational Area's entrance is a historical marker marking the site of the old Four C Sawmill, one of the largest mills of its era. The mill made Ratcliff a timber boom town in the 1920s. Some of the old sawmill ruins can be seen inside the Ratcliff Lake Recreational Area near the lake that once served as the mill's log pond.

At Ratcliff, turn north on FM 227 and proceed until you reach its intersection with Texas Highway 21—one of the oldest highways in the state. Sometimes known as El Camino Real, the Royal Highway, or the King's Highway, the road runs from Natchitoches, Louisiana, to San

Antonio and was a well-traveled route for early Texas settlers.

At Highway 21, take a right and proceed to the entrance of Mission Tejas State Park. Here, you will find a scenic park that is especially beautiful in the spring, and a couple of interesting buildings as well.

A log replica marks the site of Mission San Francisco de los Tejas, the first Spanish mission in East Texas. The mission was built by the Spanish in 1690 to stem the tide of French settlement in Texas, but later abandoned because of Indian turmoil.

Also in the park is the Rice Stagecoach Inn, one of several which once served El Camino Real. The building was started as a one-room structure in 1828, but hostile Indians forced its abandonment for two years before Joseph Raymond Rice, Sr. returned and built a substantial way station for travelers. Although Rice died in 1866, the building remained in the family until the 1970s. Mrs. Rice continued to live in the log house until her death in 1881 and other family members occupied the residence until 1919. It was moved to its site in the park in 1974.

After leaving the park, travel northward on Texas 21 until you come to an unpaved road on the right leading to the Neches River Overlook, a U.S. Forest Service recreational area. The drive to the overlook is worth the effort; the scenic view across the Neches River bottomlands is excellent.

The town of Weches, near the overlook, was originally called Neches because of its proximity to the Neches River, but when postal officials objected to putting a post office here because there was already a Neches in East Texas, a local merchant simply added another stroke to the N, making it Weches.

Return to Texas 21 and proceed south to Farm Road 227, which veers in a westerly direction. You'll travel through several interesting small communities, including Augusta, once a major farming center, until you come to Farm Road 2022. Turn south and look for a historical marker to the old Jones School House, where two generations of children learned to read and write. Also on FM 2022 is the state's largest Allegheny Chinquapin tree, about 10 miles north of Crockett on the west side of the road. The tree has a girth of about 228 inches and a height of 46 feet with a crown spread of 50 feet.

Continue south on FM 2022 until you reach an intersection with Farm Road 2663, which will carry you to Latexo. Many people who come across the name wonder if it is located on the Texas-Louisiana border, but the town simply got its odd name from the Louisiana and Texas Orchard Company, which was founded on the railroad.

At Latexo, turn south on US 287 and you'll return to Crockett.

(For more information about the places found on this Sunday Drive, contact the Crockett Chamber of Commerce, Box 307, Crockett, TX 75835, telephone 409/544-2359.)

Deep East Texas

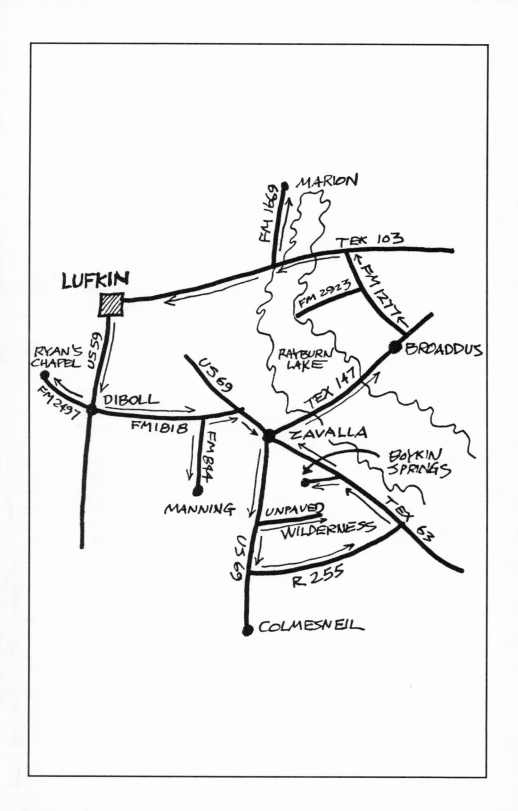

Lufkin:

Where lumbering is everything.

Here's a Sunday Drive that will provide you with a good overview of the rich logging and lumbering heritage of East Texas—along with some hefty helpings of Mexican food, hamburgers and barbecue.

The forest products industry dates back to the 1830's when the first, crudely-built sawmills—mostly men sawing logs by hand over a pit in the earth—were used to provide rough boards for the East Texas frontier. The industry began to blossom with more sophisticated mills in the 1880s when railroads like the Houston, East and West Texas Railroad began providing lumbermen with a more dependable way to ship their planks to places like Houston, Beaumont and Shreveport.

Today, Lufkin sits in the middle of the commercial forests of East Texas and most of the major industrial developments in the timber industry were realized within a 20-mile radius of the city.

Start your Sunday Drive at Lufkin, where you'll find the Texas Forestry Museum, the only museum of its kind in Texas. Located in a park-like setting on Atkinson Drive (Texas 103 west), the museum houses relics and displays from lumbering's past, including a steam logging locomotive, a log loader and railcar, and a caboose; a historic depot from Camden, a one-time company town owned by W.T. Carter and Bro. Lumber Company; a number of vehicles used at one time by other lumber companies; and an excellent collection of smaller exhibits and relics housed in a modern all-wood building.

Towering above the museum and its grounds is a full-sized forest lookout tower of the kind once used by the state's forest fire fighters as key lookouts. The fire fighters stopped using the towers years ago in favor of planes.

Also in Lufkin, make a stop at another excellent museum at the corner of Paul and Second, the Museum of East Texas, which recently completed a modern addition. The museum's exhibits rotate on a regular basis, but also provides an ongoing collection of items representative of Lufkin's early days. The museum also houses an excellent collection of East Texas art assembled by the Lufkin Rotary Club.

Just across the street from the museum near the entrance to the Lufkin Civic Center, is a statute of Angelina, the Indian maiden who helped Spanish padres bring Christianity to East Texas in the 1600s. The county of Angelina—the only Texas county bearing a woman's name—was named for the Indian maiden, who died in the 1700s and was buried somewhere near the Angelina River in neighboring Nacogdoches County.

Some other places of interest in Lufkin include Ellen Trout Park and Zoo, which includes an excellent zoo and a miniature railroad which circles the zoo and a small lake; the nearby Angelina County Exposition Center, which at one time boasted the largest clear-span indoor arena in the world, located on Loop 287 North; and Crown Colony Country Club on Highway 59 South, which boasts one of the top-rated golf courses in the state.

With a large Hispanic population, Lufkin has some of the best independently-owned Mexican food restaurants in East Texas. Our favorites are Morales, a few blocks south of downtown Lufkin on South First Street in a residential area, and Rodriquez, on Lufkin Avenue in downtown Lufkin across the street from the Ward Burke Federal Courthouse.

And, for some of the best tamales this side of the Mexican border, visit LaUnica Tortilleria on North Raguet Street. The tamales are made daily and, like most of LaUnica's foods, must be taken home to enjoy.

Lufkin is also widely known for its homestyle hamburgers. We recommend four—those at Ray's Drive-In on Timberland Drive, Cherry's Convenience Store at the intersection of 103 West and Loop 287, Thompson's Pharmacy on Ellis Avenue, and the cafeteria of Memorial Medical Center on Frank Avenue.

If you like barbecue, the best place in East Texas is also at Lufkin— Lufkin Barbecue, which serves sliced beef so tender you can cut it with a tongue depressor and spare ribs with more meat than bones. The restaurant is located on Timberland Drive at its intersection with South Chestnut.

From Lufkin, let your Sunday Drive take you south on U.S. 59 to Diboll, the corporate home of Temple-Inland Inc., one of the country's largest forest products companies. The company's corporate offices are located in a park-like setting beside U.S. 59. Stop here to see an unusual statute of an early East Texas black logger, and then drive around Loop 210 to see the old Southern Pine Lumber Company commissary store, the last of its type left in East Texas. A historical marker stands out front. Diboll is also the home of the first southern pine plywood plant built in Texas.

Just outside of Diboll, on Farm Road 2497, is Ryan's Chapel Church, dating back to 1866 when pioneer minister, Rev. Isaac Ryan, held a Methodist revival in his home before occupying it. The church's first building had puncheon seats and a dirt floor and the minister was paid in bacon, corn and syrup.

From Diboll, drive east on FM 1818. You'll pass through the Pine Grove and Beulah communities before coming to an intersection with FM 844 at Shawnee Prairie. Take a right turn and drive just up the road a few miles where you'll find a historical marker to the old sawmill town of Manning, one of the largest communities in Angelina County in the 1930s. The town's main employer, the sawmill of the Carter-Kelly Lumber Company, burned and the town became a ghost almost overnight. Only one of Manning's homes, the two-story building once used as the residence of the sawmill manager, still stands.

Return on FM 844 to FM 1818, turn right and continue until you reach the intersection with U.S. 69, turn right, and go to the town of Zavalla. Visit a while in Renfro's Arts and Crafts Store (one of the few in the region featuring pine cone arrangements and wreaths) and then take U.S. 69 south toward Woodville. A few miles before crossing the Neches River, turn left on an unpaved U.S. Forest Service road to the Upland Islands Wilderness Area, a 12,000-acre area in the Angelina National Forest. But don't look for modern conveniences; a wilderness area is a forest in the wild.

When you return to U.S. 69, proceed south past the community of Rockland and take Recreational Road 255 just north of Colmesneil. You'll be turning left. Follow the road through a gently rolling countryside until you come to its intersection with Texas 63, and then turn north back to Zavalla.

A few miles up the road, turn left on a U.S. Forest Service road leading to the Boykin Springs Recreational Area, one of the prettiest places in the East Texas woodlands. Not far from Boykin Springs is the old sawmill ghost town of Aldredge, but we recommend that you check with local Forest Service rangers for directions and advice; the zig-zagging unpaved roads are often impassable.

If you like to walk, one way to reach the old town is over the 5.5-mile Sawmill Trail, which begins at nearby Bouton Lake and ends at Boykin Springs. About midway on the trail, a 0.75-mile spur leads to the ghost town.

Return to Zavalla via 63. Look for a small roadside park on the left with a state historical marker explaining the history of the Texas National Forests and how they were created from lands cut over by gypsy timbermen around the turn of the century.

At Zavalla, turn north on Texas 147 which will take you across Sam Rayburn Lake on a mile-long bridge—the longest in East Texas. Covering some 114,500 acres, Rayburn is the largest body of water entirely within Texas and is nationally known for its bass fishing. An excellent lakeside park, Cassels-Boykin Park, lies to the west of the highway just before you reach the long bridge.

Continue on Texas 147 through the community of Broaddus to the intersection of FM 1277. Turn left here and follow the road (it passes by another lakeside park, Townsend Park, on FM 2923) until you reach Texas 103. Take another left here and follow 103 back to Lufkin. Enroute, you'll pass through the small settlement of Etoile, and one of the best small-town restaurants in the area, the Steakhouse Lantern, specializing in steaks and catfish.

After you cross over Rayburn Lake at Etoile, start looking for the intersection of FM 1669, which will take you to the site of Angelina County's first county seat, Marion, a one-time ferry crossing on the Angelina River when the county was founded in 1846.

Return to Texas 103, and just before you get back into Lufkin, look for the big Champion International papermill on the right side of the highway. Out front is a state historical marker explaining that the mill in 1940 pioneered the commercial manufacture of newsprint from southern pine trees.

(For more information about the places found on this Sunday Drive, contact the Lufkin Chamber of Commerce, 1615 South Chestnut, Box 1606, Lufkin, TX 75901, telephone 409/634-6644.)

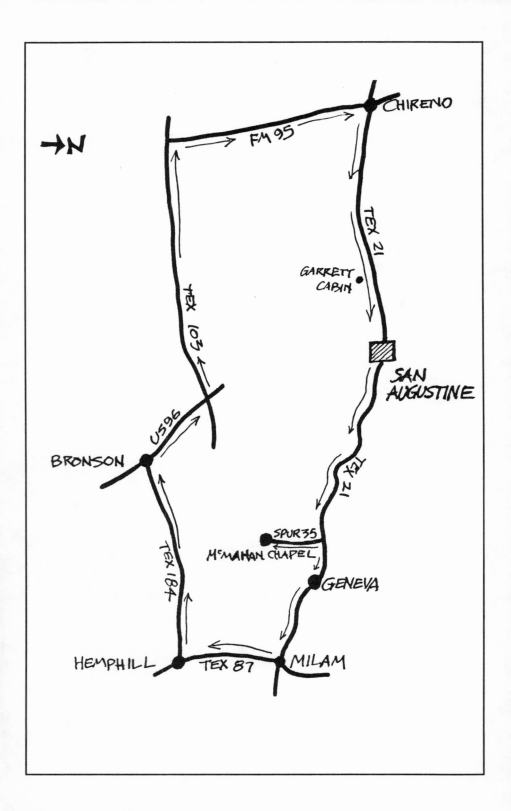

San Augustine:

Rocking the cradle of Texas.

Long before places like Houston, Dallas and Austin were even a gleam in a developer's eye, the rolling countryside around San Augustine, Hemphill and Chireno was alive with people going about the business of settling Texas.

San Augustine, in fact, calls itself "the oldest Anglo Saxon town in Texas," a slogan disputed by some of its rivals, but it has enough old buildings and homes to at least stake a partial claim on the title. Sam Houston lived here, Davy Crockett walked the town's streets, and the town's churches helped bring religious freedom to Texas—all of which enhances another Chamber of Commerce claim, "The Cradle of Texas."

Before starting your Sunday Drive, be sure to spend some time in the town. Here are a few stops worth making:

• The site of Mission Nuestra Senora de Los Delores de los Ais, which was established by Padre Fray Antonio Margil de Jesus in 1716. The mission served to confirm the claim of the King of Spain to the province of Texas. Historical markers stand about four blocks west of the courthouse square on Texas 147.

• The statute of J. Pinckney Henderson, Texas' first governor, stands on the courthouse square.

• The Ekekiel Cullen Home, built in 1839. Now used as a museum and community house, the home was given to the Daughters of the Republic of Texas in 1953 by oilman Hugh Roy Cullen, a grandson of the builder. The home is located at 205 S. Congress.

• The Colonel Stephen William Blount house, also built in 1839. This unique Greek Revival building was constructed by a signer of the Declaration of Independence. It is located at 502 S. Columbia.

• The Matthew Cartwight House, is located at 912 Main. This home was built in 1839 for Isaac Campbell and is today listed in the National Register of Historic Places.

• Christ Episcopal Church, 201 S. Ayish. The church owes its beginnings to Mrs. Frances C. Henderson, wife of J. Pinckney Henderson. The church was organized in 1848 and the present building was completed in 1870.

If you find yourself hungry in San Augustine, we recommend Doodle's Restaurant, which does a good job with homestyle meats, vegetables and breads. The chicken and dumplings are usually excellent.

From San Augustine, head east on Texas Highway 21, a route that 200 years ago carried missionaries, explorers, immigrants from the United States and soldiers across East Texas and farther west. You'll pass through the rural settlement of Ford's Corner, where Texas 21 is intersected by Farm Road 1. A lot of people think this was the first farm-to-market road built in Texas; unfortunately, it wasn't—but it was among the first such roads.

Stay on Texas 21 until you come to another intersection, this time with Spur 35. Turn right and follow the road until it deadends at McMahan Chapel, the oldest Methodist church in Texas with a continuous existence. The church was organized as a religious society in 1833 by the Rev. James Stevenson and as a church in 1834 by Rev. Henry Stepherson. Another early minister, Littleton Fowler, is buried beneath the pulpit in the church.

Return to Texas 21 and continue your Sunday Drive toward the east, passing through Geneva. The next settlement up the road is Milam, which was founded in 1828 as Red Mound, but renamed in 1835 for Benjamin Rush Milam. The town was an important seat of justice for the old Sabine Municipality in 1835 and became an important entry point for settlers coming into Texas in the 1830s.

Just east of Milam on Texas 21 is a historical monument marking the site of the Milam Masonic Institute. Many early pioneers belonged to the Ancient, Free and Accepted Masons, an order that was active in education. Among the Masons who settled in this area in 1845 were Republic of Texas leaders William Clark, James Gaines, D.S. Kaufman, Willis H. Landrum and F.M. Weatherred.

A few miles north of Milam, in the middle of the Sabine National Forest, is the Red Hills Recreational Area, an excellent place for overnight camping or a picnic. The area, just off Texas 87, is operated by the U.S. Forest Service and is one of the most attractive sites in the Sabine National Forest.

Take a turn south at Milam on Texas 87 and head for Hemphill, the easy-going county seat of Sabine County. Be sure to visit the county courthouse square, one of the most picturesque in Texas with its turn-of-the-century stores, antique and gift shops, two-story courthouse, and old county jail. The latter has been converted into a historical museum that is well worth the visit. Be sure to climb the stairs to the second floor and look over the graffiti left on the walls by thousands of prisoners. The old jail has Texas' oldest remaining gallows, still in place after 80 years, but they haven't been used in more than 60 years.

For lunch, we suggest a couple of places, the Two Sisters Restaurant, a homestyle eatery which serves an excellent plate lunch, and Twitty's, a restaurant with a more contemporary menu. Twitty's was once owned by country singer Conway Twitty.

From Hemphill, turn west on Texas 184 to Bronson, and then turn north on U.S. 96. At its intersection with Texas 103, turn west again. This scenic drive will take you through the Angelina National Forest and across Rayburn Lake. Several miles before you reach the town of Etoile, turn north on Farm Road 95 and head north to Chireno, a storybook-like village at the intersection of 95 and Texas 21.

From Chireno, return in an easterly direction to San Augustine. Just after you cross the Attoyac Bayou, look for a log cabin on the right side of the highway. It's the oldest house in San Augustine County, a cabin built in 1826 by Milton Garrett. The house stands as it was originally built with original chimneys of hand-hewn rock.

Four miles before you reach San Augustine, look for the Colonel Phillip A. Sublett house, which was actually built by Sublett's son in 1874. It is an unusual two-story home with an abundance of Ionic detail in the portico and pedimented cornices over the windows.

About a mile out of San Augustine is still another interesting landmark, the William Garrett Plantation Home, sometimes called the "House of Seven Gables." The home was built during the Civil War by slaves using hand-planed lumber and molded nails.

(For more information about the places found on this Sunday Drive, contact the San Augustine Chamber of Commerce, 132-A West Columbia, San Augustine, TX 75972, telephone 409/275-3610.)

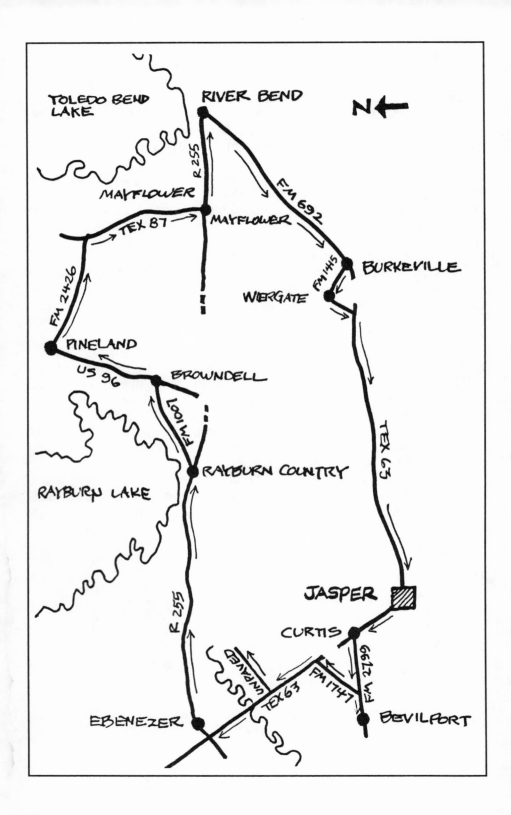

Jasper:

Wood bricks, lakes and coffee at Charlie's.

Starting at Jasper in deep East Texas, this Sunday Drive will take you on a forested tour of three counties—Jasper, Sabine and Newton—with stops at the damsites of two of Texas' largest manmade reservoirs. For good measure, we've thrown in a dash or two of sawmill history.

Before embarking on your Sunday Drive, there are several sites worth visiting in Jasper.

At the Jasper Post Office is an interesting mural painted by Alexander Levin in 1939. Called "Industries of Jasper County," the mural was part of the New Deal art program in 1934 through 1943.

At a Jasper shopping center is the Visitors Center of the Jasper Chamber of Commerce, which may be the only business building in East Texas made of wooden bricks. A hometown wood products industry introduced the wood bricks in the 1960s and built a couple of experimental homes. When the Jasper Chamber started looking around for a new building, the company donated one of the pilot homes. The wooden bricks never caught the fancy of homebuilders, but the Jasper Chamber's building continues to be one of the town's most unusual structures.

One of Jasper's most attractive homes is the Beaty-Orton gingerbread home, which was built with native pine timbers by John T. Beaty around the end of the nineteenth century. Other historic sites include the Hardy-Pace home, built in the 1830s; the Tavern Oak, a giant pin oak more than 250 years old; Dixie Baptist Church, founded in 1850 under a grove of beach trees by a black slave, Rev. Richard Seale; and the T. Gilbert Adams Memorial Pavilion, replica of an early bandstand located on the lawn of the Jasper County courthouse.

An excellent time to visit Jasper is between late March and early April when the town's azalea trail is in full bloom. Signs mark the route and you can pick up an easy-to-follow map from the Chamber of Commerce.

If you're an early riser, you'll want to have coffee at Charlie's, a Jasper cafe, where dozens of Jasper men ranging from loggers to lawyers drop in every morning between 7 and 7:45 a.m. for a free-for-all coffee break that covers almost everything. The insults flow freely and Charlie sometimes insists you'll need an asbestos bottom to sit in with the breakfast bunch. The coffee mugs, which hang on a special rack when they're not being used, bespeak the uniqueness of the bunch. They carry names like Fat Cat, Sweedie, Noodles, Poochie, Boo, Grunt, Hoo and Judge.

From Jasper, continue your Sunday Drive by heading in a northerly direction on Texas Highway 63. At the Curtis community, turn west on Farm Road 2799 and proceed to the Bevilport community. Named for John Bevil, a Texas Ranger, chief justice (county judge) of Jasper County, and a farmer, Bevilport was the forerunner of present-day Jasper. It existed in the 1830s as a shipping port on the Angelina River, sending hides, cotton, and lumber to markets in New Orleans. In 1834, it was the seat of government for the Bevil municipality. One of the most interesting homes here is the old Doom house, built by R.C. Doom, a Bevilport customs agent and tax collector. Congressman Jack Brooks owns the home and a surrounding ranch and during his presidency, Lyndon B. Johnson visited here.

From Bevilport, start back east on 2799, but turn north on Farm Road 1747 and follow it until you hit Texas 63 again. Proceed northward. Just before you cross the Angelina River, a dirt road leading to the right will carry you to the old town of De Zavala, which was named for Lorenzo de Zavala, a Mexican impresario who became a Texas patriot in the Republic of Texas fight for independence. The town, marked only by a cemetery and a historical marker, was incorporated on Christmas Eve, 1838, by an act of the Republic of Texas and was a post office until the Civil War.

When you return to Texas 63, continue north until you come to the intersection of R 255 in the Ebenezer settlement.

Not far from Ebenezer is Bean's Place, a small settlement on the Angelina River. The story goes that when Ira Bean built a store here in 1903, he named the community and its post office for James M. Horger, president of the W.H. Ford Male and Female College at nearby Newton. However, visitors and postal workers kept confusing Horger with Borger and Spurger, so the post office requested a change. The choice was Bean's Place.

At the intersection of 63 and 255, turn east on 255, crossing the dam of Sam Rayburn Reservoir, one of the largest lakes in Texas. Be sure to stop at Overlook Park, an excellent place to get a far-ranging view of the lake's lower region and the hydroelectric power plant that has been built into the dam. After leaving the dam area, continue east on 255 until you reach its intersection with Farm Road 1007, which will carry you to Browndell.

Once a sawmill town, Browndell was built in 1903 when Kirby Lumber Company established a mill about three miles southeast of

Brookeland on the banks of Mill Creek. Kirby, by then already a business legend in Texas, named the town for John Wilcox Brown, president of the Maryland Trust Company, and his wife Dell, both close friends and fellow investors in Kirby's oil and timber enterprises.

Browndell eventually attained a population of more than 1,000, but in 1925 a fire that began in a trash pile engulfed the sawmill and portions of the town. An earlier fire in 1915 had destroyed a portion of the mill, but it was quickly rebuilt. In 1925, however, the company abandoned the sawmill and Browndell's residents left to seek jobs elsewhere. Some of the old sawmill ruins can be found in the nearby forest.

From Browndell, pick up U.S. 96 to Pineland, an interesting sawmill town with some of the oldest original sawmill homes left in East Texas. Temple-Inland Inc. operates a lumber and plywood complex at Pineland and portions of the town have remained unchanged since the 1940s.

From Pineland, continue your drive in an easterly direction on Farm Road 2426 until you reach its intersection with Texas 87. Here, start south, following the route through the scenic woodlands of the Sabine National Forest. In the spring, it is one of the prettiest drives in deep East Texas. When the highway intersects with R 255 in the Mayflower community, turn east toward Toledo Bend Lake. This route will take you to the dam of the lake, which straddles the Texas-Louisiana border.

At the lake, turn south on Farm Road 692 and continue to Burkeville, where you'll want to visit the old sawmill town of Wiergate, which sits beside Farm Road 1415. Be sure to visit the Wiergate post office and look over the photographs dating back to Wiergate's existence between 1917 and 1942. At its height, the town had a population between 2,500 and 5,000 and a major sawmill.

The town had schools, churches, a community center, a commissary store where you could buy everything from tacks to caskets, a movie theater, two swimming pools, an ice plant, a uniformed baseball team, two physicians and other niceties seldom found in other sawmill towns of that era. The town died when it ran out of timber.

Farm Road 1415 will intersect with Texas 63, which will carry you back to Jasper.

For meals, we recommend several stops: Charlie's, located on U.S. 96 south of Jasper, which serves excellent barbecue, a good chicken fried steak and excellent homemade pies, and the Green Lantern in Jasper, where the seafood buffet is popular with many diners.

(For more information about the places found on this Sunday Drive, contact the Jasper Chamber of Commerce, 200 South Main, Box 638, Jasper, TX 75951, telephone 409/384-2762.)

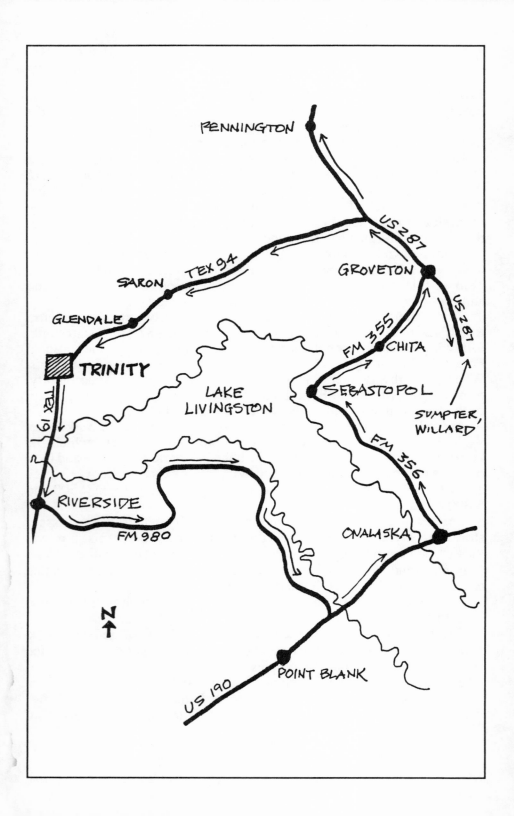

Trinity:

Sawmills and riverports.

Here's a Sunday Drive resplendent with abandoned sawmill towns and riverports, a sprinkling of other history, and more than the normal share of forest and lakefront scenery. Most of the drive is in Trinity County.

Start your Sunday Drive at Trinity, taking time to visit a number of interesting attractions. Pay special attention to Trinity's twin water towers, which loom over the downtown area. They're famous in East Texas.

In the Trinity post office is a mural painted in 1942 by artist Jerry Waters. Titled "Lumber Manufacturing," the mural is one of several scattered across East Texas, part of a unique New Deal art gallery in post offices and other public buildings.

Trinity is also the home of the now-defunct railroad, the Waco, Beaumont, Trinity and Sabine, which began as a logging train in the 1880s and ran from Trinity southward into Polk County. The little line had some of the region's most colorful nicknames during its history. Loggers called it the "Wobblety, Bobblety, Turnover and Stop." Bootleggers knew it as the "Wine, Beer, Tequila and Shinny." Housewives called it the "Wash Board, Tub and Soap." And still another sobriquet resulted from the railroad's frequent delays, "Won't be Back Till Saturday."

To continue your Sunday Drive, head south on Texas Highway 19. Just before you reach the river, you'll find the Restaurant of the River, an excellent catfish eatery, and across the river at Riverside (about a block east of Highway 19) is an equally good catfish cafe, Jake and Homer's.

When you cross the Trinity River (and the upper end of Lake Livingston) note the unusual railroad bridge to the left. The bridge was built with the ability to swing out of the way of river-going barges and vessels, but has rarely been used.

At Riverside, ask for directions to the old ghost town of Newport, on the edge of the river. Once a thriving riverport, Newport was founded in 1846 by Joseph Werner, a German immigrant and one of the wealthiest men in Walker County. At its height, Newport had a school, several churches, a post office, cotton gin, furniture factory, blacksmith shop and large general store owned by Werner. The town was abandoned with the decline of navigation on the Trinity and the arrival of the railroad in East Texas.

When you leave Newport, head in an easterly direction on Farm Road 980, which swings in an arc around Lake Livingston. Along the way, you'll find several spur roads leading to the lake's edge. Any of them will give you a good view of one of East Texas' most attractive bodies of water.

You'll also want to look out for signs leading to Waterwood, a planned settlement and country club just off FM 980. The golf course is one of the best in Texas. The restaurant here is also excellent, specializing in seafood and steaks.

FM 980 will eventually carry you to an intersection with U.S. 190 North of Point Blank. Take a left on 190 and follow it across the lake to Onalaska, a town founded by a sawmill owned by William Carlisle in 1902 and named for a town in Arkansas where Carlisle also owned a mill. The sawmill was bought by J.M. West Lumber Company, but was dismantled after West ceased operations. Drive out to the end of the Onalaska peninsula, where you'll find an interesting collection of old homes and churches.

At Onalaska, take a northern turn on FM 356. You'll pass through the old river steamboat town of Sebastopol. Look for a historical marker in front of the local store. Founded in the early 1800s by families from the town of the same name in Russia, Sebastopol was a one-time steamboat landing on the Trinity River. The town was also known as Bartholomew, which was a stop on the old Waco, Beaumont, Trinity and Sabine Railroad.

At Sebastopol, swing north toward Groveton on FM 355, a scenic route that passes through the rural settlement of Chita. In several places, the road parallels Kickapoo Creek, a pretty spring-fed stream that looks more like something from Arkansas than Texas. Rising near Groveton, the creek courses through some 25 miles before spilling into Lake Livingston. The creek includes several massive outcroppings of square-like boulders that lend credibility to the legend of an earthquake that rocked the area thousands of years ago, breaking rocks loose from a shelf beneath the earth. Most of the creek is on private land and there are few public accesses to its main body.

At Groveton, you'll find Trinity County's two-story pink brick courthouse, one of the most imposing rural courthouses in East Texas. The courthouse was built in 1914.

A few miles south of Groveton on U.S. 287 (the Corrigan highway) is the old town of Sumpter, the county's first county seat. The town, which stood in the vicinity of Sumpter Cemetery, was founded in the 1840s by farmer/merchant Solomon Adams and named for his Alabama home-town. Adams and four other settlers laid off the Sumpter townsite and later sold lots at public auction to raise money for the county's first courthouse and jail, both log buildings.

Another famous Trinity County town, Old Willard, also lies beside U.S. 287 a few miles south of Sumpter. Old Willard (now known as Woodlake) was founded by the Thompson-Tucker Lumber Company and had one of the largest sawmills in the county before it was moved to Polk County in 1910.

Further south on U.S. 287, about 8.5 miles east of Corrigan, you'll find the Bull Creek woodland trail, a 1.5-mile loop through a forest owned by Champion International. Walkers will find an abundance of large magnolias, sweet and blackgum trees, oaks and pine as it winds along the banks of Bull Creek, a clear, spring-fed stream that flows all year long. The creek bottom creates a perfect environment for a wide diversity of plant life.

At the trail, turn around and travel back to Groveton and continue your Sunday Drive by taking U.S. 287 north to Pennington, which was the county seat of Trinity County until 1882 when an election moved it to Groveton, then a blossoming sawmill town. An interesting old general store here makes the drive worthwhile.

Return south on U.S. 287 and take a right on Texas 94 toward Trinity just before the highway returns to Groveton. Texas 94 will carry you through the old sawmill town of Saron. A few sawmill ruins still stand on the townsite, a few hundred yards east of the highway in a pine thicket on property owned by a boys camp.

Just down the road is another former town, Glendale, which was founded in the 1880s by an orchard company and later settled by a religious colony. Cameron Lumber Company also operated a sawmill here.

Along the way, you'll find a scenic streamside park on White Rock Creek. It's a nice place to get a good view of some of the rock outcroppings that occur in this part of East Texas.

Wind up your Sunday Drive by continuing on 94 to Trinity, the starting place.

(For more information about the places found on this Sunday Drive, contact the Trinity Chamber of Commerce, Highway 19 South, Box 549, Trinity, TX 75862, telephone 409/594-3856, or the Groveton Chamber of Commerce, Box 366, Groveton, TX 75845, telephone 409/642-1715.)

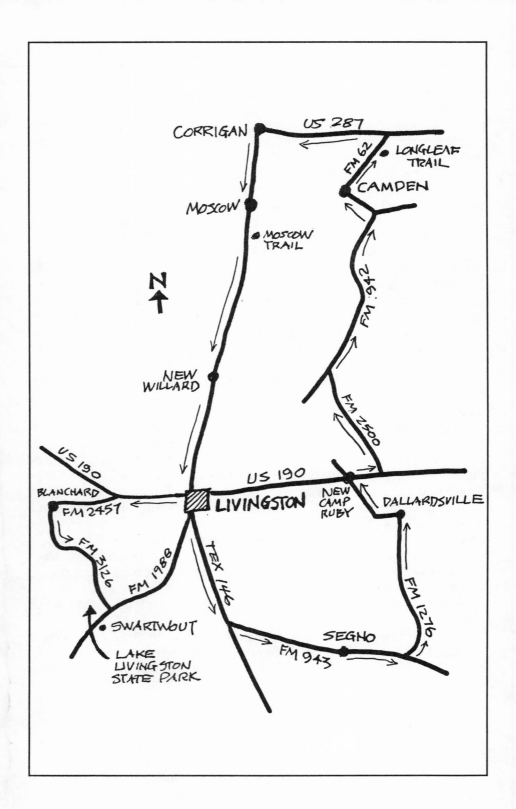

Livingston:

Tall timber, a big lake, and walking trails.

Starting at Livingston, the county seat of Polk County, this Sunday Drive will reward you with a mixture of tall timbered scenery, a look at one of the biggest lakes in Texas, a drive through the Big Thicket, and the opportunity to walk a pair of interesting woodland trails.

Before you start, spend an hour or so in Livingston. Some of the sights worth seeing include the Murphy Memorial Library and Museum, which will provide you with a good historical perspective of Polk County; a restored railroad locomotive and the Jonas Davis log cabin, both near the library; and the Polk County courthouse on the town square. Polk County was organized in 1846 and named for President James K. Polk.

Be sure to go by the local police station (a former post office) and see the rare Depression-era murals, "Buffalo Hunting" and "Landscape," which were painted by artist Theodore Van Soelen in 1940-41. The paintings were part of a government program to provide work for artists and to embellish new federal buildings.

Start your Sunday Drive by heading in a southeasterly direction on Texas 146. Near Schwab City, turn left on Farm Road 943 and follow it for several miles through the heavily forested area until you reach Segno, where a state historical marker stands as a tribute to Major Henry W. Augustine, who lost a leg in the war for Texas independence and received a large Texas land grant.

From Segno, continue east and then swing north on FM 1276, which will carry you to Dallardsville, a community sometimes known as Big Sandy for its high school featuring Indian basketball stars from the nearby Alabama-Coushatta reservation (see the Woodville tour). From Dallardsville, proceed north on 1276 through portions of the Big Thicket National Preserve's Big Sandy Creek unit.

Stay on 1276 and you'll hit U.S. 190 at New Camp Ruby. Turn east toward the Alabama-Coushatta Indian Reservation and then veer north again on FM 2500.

You'll eventually intersect FM 942 at Cedar Grove, where you should turn right toward Camden, once an old-time sawmill settlement built around the W.T. Carter and Bro. Lumber Company. The company was sold in the 1960s to Champion International, which today operates a plywood and stud complex at Camden. Camden is also served by one of the shortest railroad lines in the state, the Moscow, Camden and San Augustine, a 5.5-mile line running between Camden and Moscow. Most of the old W.T. Carter buildings at Camden have been relocated or destroyed; the lone exception is the old office building, which is still used by Champion.

From Camden, take FM 62. About three miles north of Camden is the Longleaf Pine Trail, a woodland hiking trail through one of several stands of virgin longleaf pine left in East Texas. Many of the trees along the trail are 100 years old and older, and some are home to the rare, red-cockaded woodpecker. The trail is located on land owned by International Paper Company.

When you leave the trail, continue on FM 62 to its intersection with U.S. 287, turn west and proceed to Corrigan. From here, start south on U.S. 59 until you reach the Moscow community, where gunfighter John Wesley Hardin killed his first man before he was 15. Moscow was also the birthplace of William P. Hobby, a former Texas governor (a small park and historical marker is found beside U.S. 59).

About a mile south of Moscow on U.S. 59 is the Moscow Woodland Trail, where you'll find a pleasant stroll through an old-growth forest managed by Champion.

Proceed south on U.S. 59 until you reach the community of New Willard, where a spur highway will carry you past the old sawmill settlement. The town was established in 1910 when the Thompson-Tucker Lumber Company at Old Willard (between Corrigan and Groveton) exhausted its timber and moved to Freeman seven miles north of Livingston, renaming the location New Willard. The sawmill closed down in the 1950s.

From New Willard, continue on U.S. 59 into Livingston and then veer west on U.S. 190 toward Lake Livingston, a huge 82,600-acre reservoir sprawling over four counties and stretching some 52 miles long.

For one of the most attractive lakeside drives on the lake, leave U.S. 190 where it intersects with FM 2457, proceed through the Blanchard community, and then follow FM 3126 around the lake shoreline until you arrive at Lake Livingston State Park, a good spot for a picnic or overnight camp. The park covers some 640 acres on the shoreline.

FM 1988 near the park will carry you south to the Lake Livingston Dam, where you'll find an excellent overlook. Nearby is a historical monument marking the site of the old town of Swartwout, which was founded on the Trinity River in 1838 by three promoters, Arthur Garner,

Thomas Bradley and James Morgan. They envisioned a prosperous trading center on the river and, at the suggestion of friend Sam Houston, they persuaded Samuel Swartwout, a New York politician and financier, to invest in their venture. The town, however, died when the railroad came to East Texas and steamboats stopped using the river and lumbermen ceased floating their branded logs south to Galveston.

Not far from the old town is the Southland Park Cafe, where the house specialty is the fresh catfish caught daily from the Trinity River.

From the Lake Livingston dam, FM 1988 will carry you back to Livingston. Nearby is a state historical marker to paddlewheel boats on the Trinity, once the most navigable of Texas' winding, debris-choked rivers. Of 17 riverboat landings in Polk County, Swartwout, Smithfield and Drew's Landing were three of the most important. At times, eight or more steamboats, stern and side-wheelers, could be seen at a busy landing. Although the Trinity played a leading role in Texas commerce between 1840 and 1900, railroads eventually ended the steamboat era.

(For more information about the places found on this Sunday Drive, contact the Livingston Chamber of Commerce, 516 West Church, Street, Livingston, TX 77351, telephone 409/327-4929.)

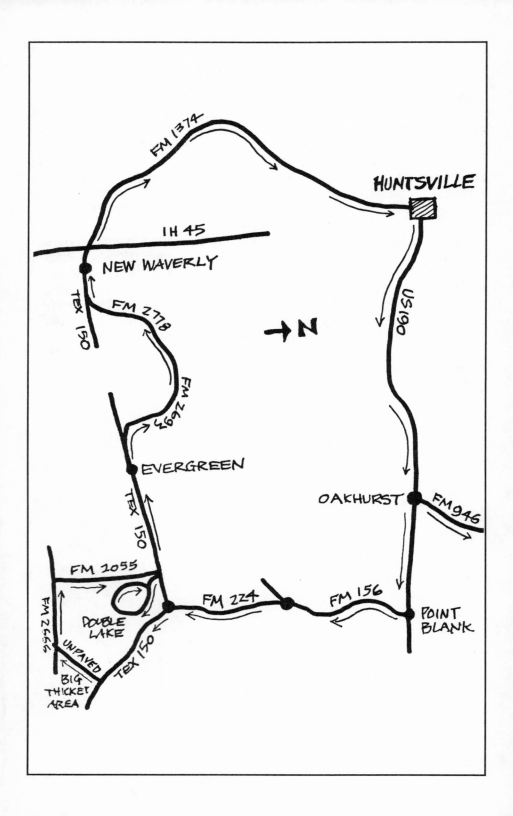

Huntsville:

Old Sam, prisons and pine trees.

If you're an admirer of General Sam Houston—the respected and sometimes-cursed maker of Texas history—this Sunday Drive is just for you. The drive will also take you through a good portion of the Sam Houston National Forest and along the shoreline of Lake Livingston.

Start at Huntsville, and spend some time in the town before you launch your Sunday Drive. An excellent guide is the Huntsville Fun Trail, a publication you can pick up at the local Chamber of Commerce office.

Some of the local stops you'll want to touch include the Sam Houston Memorial Grave and Monument in Oakwood Cemetery. Since 1911, an impressive monument inscribed with the promise that "the world will take care of Houston's fame" has marked the grave of the first President of the Republic of Texas. The cemetery can be reached by traveling down the two blocks of Spur 94, the shortest highway in Texas, which intersects Texas 190.

Some other stops we suggest:

• The Sam Houston Memorial Park and Museum, just off U.S. 75 (Sam Houston Avenue). Here in a 15-acre setting are Sam Houston's home, "Woodland," the steamboat house where he died in 1863, his law office, a pioneer kitchen, a blacksmith shop and other buildings. The museum itself houses one of the most extensive collections of Sam Houston memorabilia in Texas.

• The Walls, the original main unit of the Texas prison when all of its prisoners were housed here. The massive red brick walls front on U.S. 190. Near the Walls is a museum housing prison exhibits, including an electric chair once used for excutions in Texas.

• Peckerwood Hill (Captain Joe Byrd Cemetery), the final resting place for more than 900 prisoners whose bodies were unclaimed at the time of their death. The 22-acre graveyard is on Bowers Boulevard just off Sam Houston Avenue. Look for interesting markers.

• The Thorwaldsen Statute of Christ in Oakwood Cemetery. The copy of the famous Thorwaldsen original in Copenhagen, Denmark, was placed here by Judge and Mrs. Ben Powell as a monument to their son.

• Emancipation Park, a landmark of freedom for Texas slaves, where Juneteenth is celebrated each year.

• The Ahysen Mural in downtown Huntsville. Depicting Huntsville in the spring, the 938-square foot mural—called the largest free-standing painting in the United States—was done in ceramics by art professor Harry Ahysen.

• The Gibbs Bros. building, a Huntsville landmark dating back to the 1840s when Thomas and Sandford Gibbs opened the store and later entered the banking business. Today, Gibbs heirs constitute the oldest business in Texas under original ownership at the same location on the Huntsville courthouse square.

If you're hungry before you leave town, we recommend a couple of eating places, the Cafe Texan on the courthouse square, which has been serving an excellent pepper steak for some 50 years, and the Junction, an old plantation home (it was built as a wedding gift to a bride in 1849) that has been turned into an excellent restaurant.

From Huntsville, start east on U.S. 190. You'll pass through the town of Oakhurst, which was once a thriving sawmill town in San Jacinto County. A sawmill at Palmetto was moved to Oakhurst in 1911 and operated for a number of years. The town was named for Oakhurst, Oklahoma, home of several lumbermen who had moved to Texas.

Continuing on U.S. 190, some three miles north of Oakhurst, about two miles off FM 946, is Sam Houston's country home, Raven Hill, a name taken from the Cherokee Indians' name for Houston, "The Raven." A Texas historical marker is all that remains on the site.

Just east of Oakhurst is the entrance to Waterwood National Country Club, one of the best golf courses in Texas. The course offers 18 rugged holes built in the old Scottish tradition.

A little farther up U.S. 190 you'll discover the village of Point Blank, which sounds like something out of an Old West novel. Actually, Point Blank was originally named Blanc Point by a Frenchwoman who moved here from Alabama. The town was also known as Point White and White Point. Ask for directions to a small cemetery on the banks of Lake Livingston, where Texas' second governor, George T. Wood, is buried.

Lake Livingston, covering some 82,600 acres, sprawls over several East Texas counties and is popular with fishermen, boaters and campers.

From Point Blank, take Texas 156 southward along the banks of the lake. Near Holiday Shores, turn on FM 224, which will carry you into Coldspring, the county seat of San Jacinto County since 1870. Spend some time in the quaint shops around the courthouse square and be sure to visit the courthouse, as well as the old county jail, now an excellent small-town museum.

Coldspring has had several other names during its lifetime, including Cookskin, Fireman's Hill and Cold Spring.

From Coldspring, head south on Texas 150 toward Shepherd, but a few miles out of Coldspring, take a right turn onto a unpaved road leading to the Big Creek Scenic Area, a tangled forest area that offers a good insight to what the Big Thicket looks like. The actual Thicket is 30 to 40 miles east of the area.

Continue on the unpaved road until it intersects with FM 2666 and follow this highway until you come to its intersection with FM 2055. Turn north and head back toward Coldspring, but a few miles out of town, look for the signs to the Double Lake Recreational Area, one of the most popular parks in the Sam Houston National Forest. The area offers facilities for camping, hiking, picnicking and fishing.

When you leave Double Lake, turn north until you come to Texas 150. Turn west toward New Waverly and you'll pass through the small settlement of Evergreen. Along the way, look for the entrance to the Lone Star Hiking Trail, the longest (140 miles) of its kind in the state. The trail traverses the entire Sam Houston National Forest and crosses two developed camping areas, Double Lake and Stubblefield Lake.

At the intersection of 150 and FM 2693 in the Pleasant Grove settlement, turn north on the farm road and follow it until it turns into FM 2778, which will lead back to an intersection with Texas 150, which will carry you to New Waverly.

At New Waverly, turn west on FM 1374, which will take you on a wide loop carrying you through some of the tallest timberland in the Huntsville area. Stay on the road, passing through Bethel and Union Hill, and you'll wind up in Huntsville.

However, before leaving Huntsville, take the time to drive south on Interstate 45, and look for the turnoff to two other places you'll want to visit before completing this drive:

• Huntsville State Park, a 2,000-acre park with hiking and biking trails, paddle boats, screened shelters, and campsites overlooking scenic Raven Lake.

• Elkins Lake. Here, be sure to drive slowly through one of Huntsville's most prestigious residential areas with a peaceful lake, rolling hills, winding streets, and thousands of tall pines, all complemented by Judge Elkins' spacious log Manor House, now a country club.

(For more information about the places found on this Sunday Drive, contact the Huntsville Chamber of Commerce, 1328 11th Street, Box 538, Huntsville, TX 77340, telephone 409/295-8113.)

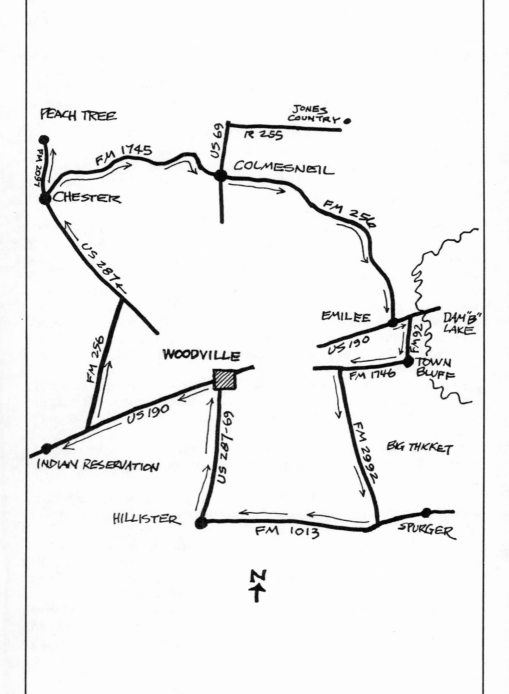

PEACH TREE

FM 1745

FM 2097

CHESTER

US 287

FM 256

WOODVILLE

US 190

INDIAN RESERVATION

US 287-69

HILLISTER

JONES COUNTRY

US 69

R 255

COLMESNEIL

FM 256

EMILEE

US 190

DAM "B" LAKE

FM 92

TOWN BLUFF

FM 1746

BIG THICKET

FM 2992

FM 1013

SPURGER

N

Woodville:

Dogwoods, cornbread and indians.

The best time for this Sunday Drive is in early spring when the dog-woods begin threading blossoms through the forests of Tyler County.

On the last weekend of March and the first weekend of April, Woodville hosts the annual Dogwood Festival, which pays tribute to the arrival of springtime in East Texas. The events include a parade, historical pageant, a western trailride and rodeo.

An excellent side trip out of Woodville is the Dogwood Walking Trail, three miles east of Woodville off U.S. 190. Winding along the banks of Theuvenin Creek, the trail is noted for dogwood blooms in the spring. It is maintained by International Paper Company and spans about 1.5 miles.

To start your Sunday Drive, begin in Woodville and spend some time at Heritage Village, a community of authentic pioneer buildings unlike anything in East Texas. Located just west of Woodville on U.S. 190, the village is a good place to pick up the flavor of early East Texas. You'll find a working blacksmith shop, a country store, an old farm kitchen, a rural post office and other buildings dating back to the turn-of-the-century.

You'll also find in the Village one of our favorite restaurants in East Texas, the Pickett House. Homestyle boarding house meals are served on long, oilcloth-covered tables. The Pickett House is actually a 75-year-old schoolhouse that was moved to Heritage Village and turned over to some of the best cooks in Texas. The house specialty is chicken-and-dumplings and fresh cornbread made from meal ground in the village.

Another place worth visiting in Woodville is the Allen Shivers Museum, just two blocks north of the Tyler County Courthouse. The museum, open on weekdays and Saturdays, contains memorabilia of the former Texas governor and statesman who grew to boyhood in Woodville.

When you leave Woodville, continue west on 190 to the Alabama-Coushatta Indian Village. The village is located on Park Road 56 just off the main highway. Special tour buses are available to carry visitors into the lush forest and through historical sites with narration by the guides. A miniature train also runs through the Big Thicket.

The reservation—one of only two such reservations in Texas--also offers demonstrations by skilled Indian craftsmen, samples of authentic Indian foods, intriguing stories of Alabama-Coushatta legends, colorful tribal dances and demonstrations with reptiles.

The residents of the reservation, while they live in the Big Thicket, have never lived in tents and spent most of their lives as hunters and gatherers, not fighters. History has a high regard for the Indians, who were almost wiped out by smallpox and other diseases in the early decades of the 20th century. Today, the tribe numbers about 550 and two of its 12 clans have died out. But those who remain on the reservation preserve their language and customs.

When you return to 190, head east toward Woodville and then veer north on Farm Road 256 and follow it through the thick pine forests until it intersects with U.S. 287. Then head north to the community of Chester.

At Chester, take FM 2097 about two miles to the Peach Tree settlement, the boyhood home of famous Texas timberman John Henry Kirby, son of John Thomas Kirby, who settled here in the 1850s and raised his family, including John Henry, in a log cabin. After he achieved wealth and national influence as a lawyer, oilman and timberman, Kirby built at Peach Tree an elaborate brick chapel to honor his parents. The chapel was dedicated in 1913 by Kirby's old friend, Congressman Samuel Bronson Cooper, and the timberman went to considerable expense to have a Russian artist, Boris Bernard Gordon, paint a wall-sized mural of his father's Baptism in a nearby pond. The painting was so lifelike when it was unveiled that Tyler County residents regularly visited the chapel to pick out familiar faces in the Baptismal crowd. The chapel is maintained today as a museum to Kirby and is owned by a church group.

After visiting Peach Tree Village, return to Chester and take FM 1745 toward Colmesneil, but be sure to stop on the way to visit Mount Hope Cemetery, a few miles out of Chester. The cemetery is famous for its "history book monument," a shaft of granite containing 218 words, 15 historical dates, and the names of 13 individuals. They tell the story of pioneer farmer James Barnes' family, founders of Mount Hope Methodist Church. The cemetery also contains a granite mausoleum, a tribute to the Barnes family.

Just out of Chester, reached only by logging routes which are often difficult to travel, is the ghost town of Fort Teran, a Mexican outpost built on a bluff of the Neches River by General Mier y Teran to check American colonization in Texas. Marked by a state historical marker, the bluff is one of the prettiest sites in East Texas, but one of the most difficult to reach. Ask for directions in Chester before you undertake the journey.

As you continue on FM 1745, you will reach Colmesneil. Just north of the town is the Jones Country Music Park, built by country singer George

Jones on a 200-acre forested site. To reach the park, take U.S. 69 north from Colmesneil, take a right on Recreational Road 255 and go five miles.

Back in Colmesneil, continue your Sunday Drive by turning onto FM 256, which will carry you to Tejas Lake, a few miles east of the community. The lake is shaped like the outline of Texas and is a popular swimming, boating and picnicking area in the spring and summer.

On FM 256, you will pass through the tall-timbered, gently-rolling countryside to the settlement of Emilee on U.S. 190 near Steinhagen Lake. Emilee, founded in the 1880s, was once (under the name of Wolf Creek) a potential county seat for Tyler County. Sam Houston once visited here and was given a large cake baked by the settlement's women. Founded by Wyatt Hanks, the town had a post office in 1885 but was a ghost town by 1949.

Continue on 190 toward Steinhagen Lake, also known locally as Town Bluff Lake and Dam B Lake. The lake covers some 13,700 acres and around its shoreline is a popular state park, Martin Dies Jr. State Park.

Before crossing the lake, take a right on FM 92, which runs south along the lake's western shoreline. Look out for the community of Town Bluff, another settlement founded by riverman Wyatt Hanks with a ferry across the Neches River. In 1837, A.C. and J.K. Allen, the founders of Houston, bought 640 acres of land here and had considered the site for a new town. Once known as "the Natchez on the Neches," Town Bluff was the home of many early Tyler County leaders and the temporary county seat of the county when it was founded in 1846.

While on FM 92, look for a small park which overlooks the lake's dam and spillway. The view from the park is spectacular.

At Town Bluff, take a westerly turn on FM 1746 and in the Antioch community, turn south on FM 2992, which will lead you to one of the units of the Big Thicket National Biological Preserve. The preserve contains a number of units such as this, each a ecological pocket of birds, animals and rare plant life. A ranger is usually on duty at the Big Thicket's North District office on Pine Street in Woodville, and it's a good idea to pick up a map to acquaint yourself with the area.

Continue on FM 2992 and it will carry you to FM 1013. Proceed west to the community of Hillister, where you will find an excellent countrystyle restaurant, The Homestead, housed in a former residence built in 1913 by Mr. and Mrs. O.A. Norton. The rooms are furnished in antiques and collectables and the menu features several excellent dishes, including a chicken fried steak once featured in Texas Highways Magazine.

From Hillister, turn north on U.S. 69 back to Woodville.

(For more information about the places found on this Sunday Drive, contact the Woodville Chamber of Commerce, 507 North Pine Street, Woodville, TX 75979, telephone 409/283-2632.)

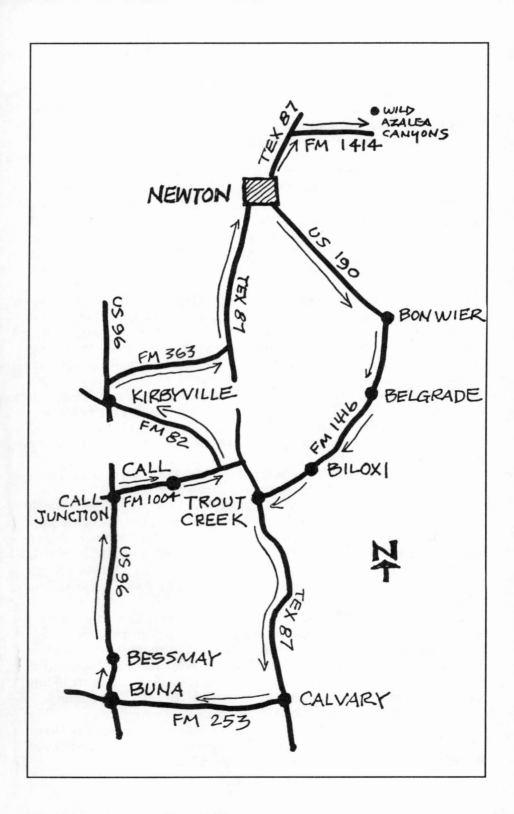

Newton:

A drive through Kirby country.

Timber magnate John Henry Kirby left a long legacy in East Texas—
and this Sunday Drive will take you through much of "Kirby country."
Enroute, you'll visit some of Kirby's old sawmill towns and pass through
some of the deepest woods in East Texas.

Start your tour at Newton, where you'll find one of the most interesting
courthouses in East Texas. Pay attention to the large clock at the top of the
edifice, a state historical landmark.

About a block off the courthouse square is the Newton Civic Center,
which also houses an excellent small-town museum worth a visit. Many
of the relics are from the days when Newton County—located on "the old
Beef Trail"—was a supply and military center for the Civil War and a
target for federals trying to take Texas. A military campground with
corrals furnishing fresh stagecoach teams and shops for tanning leather
for military boots and shoes was located on Cow Creek.

Newton and Newton County were named for Corporal John Newton,
1752-1807, a hero of the American Revolution.

One of East Texas' most attractive woodland areas, the Wild Azalea
Canyons, is near Newton, and the best time to visit the area is in March
and April when the canyons bloom with pale pink flowers. To reach the
trail, drive 4.4 miles north of Newton on Texas 87, then 6.7 miles east on
Farm Road 1414. Hikers must cover another 1.8 miles of unpaved road to
reach the entrance. Once you reach the area, you'll find yourself in a
pocket wilderness of longleaf pines, rock cliffs and wild azaleas.

To continue your Sunday Drive, return to Newton and start south on
U.S. 190 to Bon Wier. Once a thriving logging and sawmill town, Bon
Wier today is a shell of its former self. The town was built in 1905 as a
station on the Jasper and Eastern Railroad to serve the Trotti and Lee
sawmill and was named for B.F. Bonner and R.W. Wier, officials of the
Kirby Lumber Company. Surrounded by dense forests then and now, Bon
Wier was the site of three Kirby logging camps.

At Bon Wier, continue south through the Sabine River bottomlands on

Farm Road 1416, passing near the old Belgrade settlement, once a Republic of Texas port of entry on the Sabine River. William McFarland and his son, Thomas, laid out the town in 1837 on the river's bluffs. The town grew as a result of steamboat traffic on the Sabine and its proximity to the Coushatta Trace, one of the busiest mainland routes into early Texas. During its declining years, one of Belgrade's residents, Jack Johnson, the great black heavyweight boxer, gained fame with his exploits. Most accounts say that Johnson came from Galveston, but he also lived and worked as a logger and riverboat hand at Belgrade.

From Belgrade, continue south on 1416 through the Biloxi settlement and the intersection with Texas 87 at Trout Creek. Biloxi was established on the site of an old Indian village on Cow Creek in the early 1800s. It had a post office between 1857 and 1867; legend says the town was named for Biloxi, Mississippi, because several families came from there.

At Trout Creek, head south on Texas 87 until you come to the intersection of Farm Road 253 at Calvary. Turn west on 253 and follow it until you reach Buna.

Buna was founded in 1892 as a logging camp for the Beaumont Lumber Company on the old Gulf, Colorado and Sante Fe Railroad. A tram railroad was built 10 miles southwest to Ford's Bluff, from which logs were floated down the Neches River to the company's Beaumont mill. First named Carrolla for the Carroll family of Beaumont, the town was later renamed for Buna Corley, a cousin of Joe E. Carroll Sr., the logging manager.

The town and its installations were bought by Kirby Lumber Company in 1901 and continued to serve as a logging camp until 1909.

Just north of Buna, the lumber company built a large sawmill in the early 1900s, naming it for Bessmay Kirby, the only daughter of John Henry Kirby. The sawmill, however, burned in 1949.

Bessmay lies just off U.S.96 north of Buna. From Bessmay, continue on 96 until you reach Call Junction, where you should turn eastward on Farm Road 1004 to old Call, site of another Kirby Lumber Company sawmill in the early 1900s. The town was founded on the Orange and Northeastern Railroad and named for Dennie Call, a business associate of the town's founder, George Adams, Sr. The Cow Creek Tram Company built Call's first sawmill in 1895 and it was acquired by Kirby in 1901. Call lies on the border of Newton and Jasper counties and today is virtually a ghost town.

A few miles east of Call, turn north on Farm Road 82, which will take you through the E.O. Siecke State Forest, the first such forest established in Texas and noted for its scenic, ramrod-stiff pine trees. Consisting of about 1,722 acres in Newton County, the land was purchased in 1924 and additions were made in 1946. Mr. Seicke was a former director of the

Texas Forest Service.

After leaving the Siecke forest, stay on FM 82, which will carry you to Kirbyville, a town named for John Henry Kirby in 1895. The townsite was laid out by Kirby and R.P. Allen and a sawmill was built in 1896 by the Coon and Withers Lumber Company. It later became a part of the Kirby empire and was destroyed by a fire in 1917.

From Kirbyville, take Farm Road 363, which intersects U.S. 96 just north of the town. FM 363 will carry you to the intersection of Texas 87, which will led you back to Newton.

If you find yourself hungry during your trip, we suggest The Little House at Kirbyville, which offers one of the best plate lunches in this part of East Texas. The cooks also do an excellent job with homemade pies, especially the chocolate.

(For additional information about the places on this Sunday Drive, contact the Newton Chamber of Commerce, Box 66, Newton, TX 75966, telephone 409/379-5527, and the Kirbyville Chamber of Commerce, Box 417, Kirbyville, TX 75956, telephone 409/423-2451.)

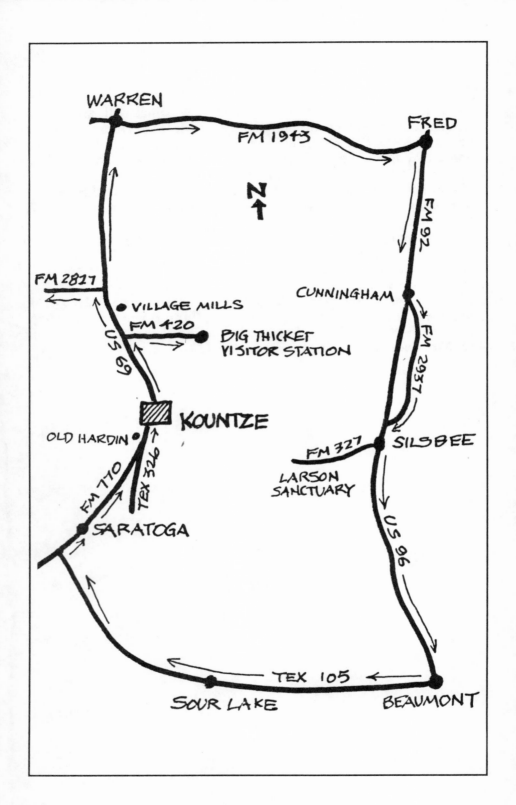

Kountze:

Roaming around in the Big Thicket.

The Big Thicket has intrigued visitors for decades, and this Sunday Drive will take you into the heart of the land of baygalls, swamps, lush forests and sawmill ghost towns.

Start your Sunday Drive at Kountze, the Hardin County seat which calls itself "the Big Light in the Big Thicket." Head north on U.S. 69 and take a right on Farm Road 420, which winds along the southern edge of the Big Thicket's Turkey Creek unit. Here, you'll find a Big Thicket information center, which is open daily in the summer and on weekends in the winter. Be sure to pick up a Big Thicket map and informational brochure; they will make your drive a lot easier.

Head back to U.S. 69 and continue north until you come to Village Mills, a ghost town. Village Mills died in the 1940s when its post office was moved, but the death knell was really sounded a decade earlier when the town's sawmill—one of the largest in Hardin County—blew its last work whistle.

At its peak in the 1890s the sawmill broke the world's record for lumber production by cutting 255,000 board feet in 11 hours on a single circular saw, some 65,000 feet above the previous record. Some lumber producers quickly questioned the accuracy of the Village Mills claim, and it took sworn affidavits before a Hardin County judge to settle the record.

W.A. Fletcher and John W. Keith built the Village Mills sawmill in 1881 and it was bought by John Henry Kirby in 1904. At one time the town had 800 residents, 400 of whom worked for the Kirby mill.

Remain on U.S. 69 until you reach the intersection of Farm Road 2827. Take a left and you'll be in the Big Thicket's Hickory Creek savannah, one of the smallest units in the preserve. After your visit here, return to U.S. 69 and proceed north to Warren, where you should turn eastward on Farm Road 1943, which will carry you across the top of the Turkey Creek unit and through the settlements of Midway and Mt. Nebo. When you reach the intersection with Farm Road 92 at Fred, head south.

In the Cunningham community, take a left turn onto Farm Road 2937, which will carry you along the western edge of the Big Thicket's Neches Bottom and Jack Gore Baygall. Several unpaved roads will carry you deeper into the units, but make sure the roads are passable.

If you remain on 2937, you'll wind up back on Farm Road 92 and eventually come to Silsbee, Hardin County's largest community. Founded in 1894 by John Henry Kirby as a sawmill town, Silsbee's fortunes are still tied to the lumbering industry. The Silsbee Little Theater is one of the best-known amateur groups in East Texas and Silsbee offers excellent city parks for a picnic and Sunday Drive rest stop. Of special interest is the eight-acre Red Cloud Water Park with a spring-fed lake and white sandy beach.

Four miles west of Silsbee on Farm Road 327 is the Roy E. Larsen Sandyland Sanctuary, a Texas Nature Conservatory Preserve of 2,138 acres. The area is a curious intermingling of various forest and wetland communities Of special interest is the sandylands where desert plants such as prickley pear cactus and yucca are found with longleaf pines and drought-resistant oak. Rare orchids and carnivorous plants also grow here among acid-loving ferns and sphagnum moss.

Village Creek, one of the prettiest streams in the Big Thicket, flows through the sanctuary, providing an enjoyable canoeing experience.

From Silsbee, continue south on U.S. 96, crossing the Little Pine Island Bayou corridor before you enter Beaumont.

In Beaumont, turn in a westerly direction on Texas 105 and head for Sour Lake, a town which attracted such early Texans as General Sam Houston because of its mineral springs that had been used for years by Indians. One spring's water, with high sulfuric acid content, primed telegraph batteries during the Civil War. This was of vital importance because telegraph service, at best, was limited.

When oil was discovered here in 1901, the Sour Lake Oil Field became one of the most prolific fields in the state, producing some 90 million barrels up to 1948. The Texas Company—now known as Texaco—was founded here and still owns property around the community.

Continue with your drive on 105 until you reach the intersection with Farm Road 770 and head for Saratoga. Settled a decade before the Civil War, Saratoga was named for Saratoga, New York, because of medicinal springs found before the turn of the century. The town, however, declined as a health resort when oil was discovered in 1901.

Saratoga is also the home of the Big Thicket Museum, which houses backwoods memorabilia from butter molds to logging equipment, pioneer artifacts and documents, a 19th century log cabin, and interpretive material on the Big Thicket flora and fauna.

Not far from Saratoga is the Bragg Road, where the ghost light of the Big Thicket has floated up and down the road for more than a century.

Some say it's the spirit of a decapitated railroader looking for his head. Others insist the light is the spectral fire pan of a night hunter who lost his way in the Big Thicket years ago and still searches for a way out. And there's still another legend of a Mexican track crew murdered and buried in the woods.

Scientists offer two less ethereal explanations. One, the light may be caused by a form of gas commonly found in swampy areas or, two, it could be the reflection of automobile headlights rounding a bend on the county road. Whatever the reason for the blob-like light that appears without warning on the arrow-straight road, it attracts a lot of attention. People wander into Hardin County from as far away as Dallas, hoping to catch a glimpse.

The Bragg Road turns left off Farm Road 1293 about seven miles west of Honey Island and heads straight for Saratoga. It's a dirt road but usually well-graded and ditched.

Stay on 770 at Saratoga and you'll wind up at the intersection with Texas 326 at Old Hardin, which was founded as Hardin County's first county seat in 1859. The town prospered until it was bypassed by the Sabine and East Texas Railroad in 1881. A fire of suspicious origin destroyed the courthouse in 1886 and in an election a year later, Kountze, on the railroad, was named the county seat.

Continue on Texas 326, which will carry you back to Kountze where you began your Sunday Drive. Along 770 and 326 is the Big Thicket's Lance Rosier unit, one of the largest parts of the preserve.

For lunch, we recommend the Pilgrim House Restaurant at Kountze, which prides itself on old-fashioned home cooking. The chicken and dumplings and barbecued ribs are house specialties, and a favorite of local diners is the pepper steak.

Another good eatery is the Lumber Company in Silsbee, which offers a downhome menu consisting of barbecue, chicken, roast beef and the like. The restaurant also offers a weekly seafood buffet.

(For more information about the places found on this Sunday Drive, contact the Kountze Chamber of Commerce, Box 878, Kountze, TX 77625, telephone 409/246-2761, or the Silsbee Chamber of Commerce, 835 Highway 96 South, Silsbee, TX 77656, telephone 409/385-5562.)

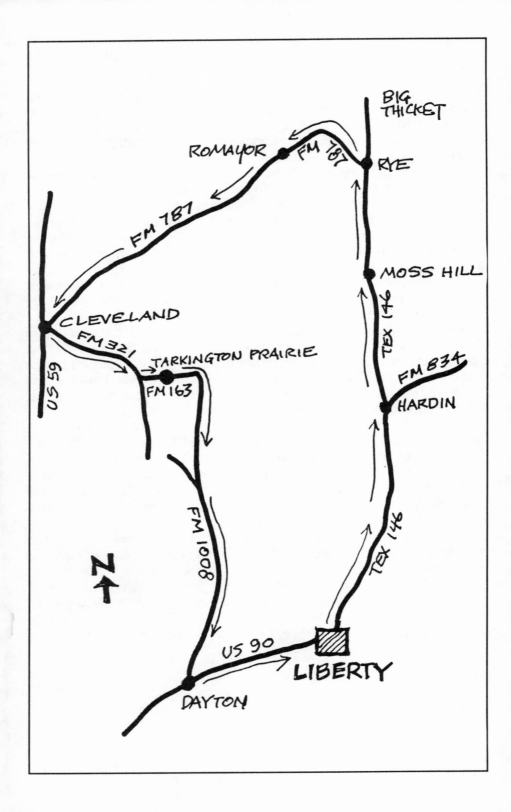

Liberty:

The land known as Atascosita.

In 1757, most of Southeast Texas was known as Atascosita, a broad timbered area that attracted thousands of Anglo settlers from the United States.

This Sunday Drive will carry you through the heart of the old Atascosita District, including Liberty, Liberty County, portions of the Big Thicket, Cleveland and several other towns.

Start your Sunday Drive at Liberty, which traces its origins to the 1750s when the Spanish, hoping to prevent French trade with the Indians, established an outpost called Atascosita near the point where an Indian trail crossed the Trinity River.

In 1831, a municipality was established in the area on the old John M. Smith plantation. The official title given to the muncipality was "Villa de La Santissima Trinidad de las Libertad (City of the Blessed Trinity of Liberty)." The town of Liberty was incorporated in 1837 and has remained a county seat since.

Liberty is filled with interesting historical sites. Here are a few of them:

• The Sam Houston Regional Library and Research, located about four miles northeast of Liberty on Farm Road 1011. The center houses archives from the 10 counties which made up the original Atascosita District. Also on the grounds is the home of Texas Governor Price Daniel, a replica of the Governor's Mansion in Austin.

• The Geraldine D. Humpreys Cultural Center, which houses an excellent regional historical museum. Also on the site is an exact replica of the Liberty Bell.

• The courthouse square, set aside as Plaza de Casa Constitorial in 1831.

• Sam Houston Plaza, site of Sam Houston's law office when he lived in the area.

• Champ de'Asile, the "haven of refuge" for nearly 400 Napoleonic exiles led by General Charles Lallemand, who settled here for a short time in the 1800s.

From Liberty, continue your Sunday Drive by heading north on Texas 146. At the settlement of Hardin, take a side trip of about three miles east on Farm Road 834 to see the largest holly tree in North America. The tree measures some 53 feet tall and has a crown spread of about 61 feet.

Continue north on 146 and just before you reach Moss Hill, look for a historical marker to Kalita, the chief of the Coushatta Indians. He helped Anglo settlers in their escape from Santa Anna's army during the Runaway Scrape of 1836.

Also on 146, north of Moss Hill, you'll find another monument marking the site of Grand Cane, the home of Sam Houston from 1843 to 1845 when he was serving a second term as president of the Republic of Texas. Grand Cane was a steamboat port on the Trinity River.

In the community of Rye, turn on Farm Road 787 toward Romayer. However, before you make the turn, you may want to continue a few miles north on 146 until you reach the Menard Creek Corridor unit of the Big Thicket National Biological Preserve. The corridor, which preserves a scenic creek that runs through the Big Thicket, contains vegetation not usually found in other parts of East Texas.

Back on 787, as you travel west, you'll pass through the community of Romayor, which dates its origin back to the 1700s when Joaquin F. de Rumayor acquired a land grant. Several sawmills once operated in the heavily forested area, but Romayor is best known for the Trinity Valley Chemurgic Institute, which once tried to develop industrial products from castor beans, moss and other Big Thicket growth.

Continue on 787 to Cleveland, a town built by the Houston East and West Texas Railroad in 1878 when the railroad started its push through East Texas. For the sum of a dollar and the privilege of having the town named for him, Charles Lander Cleveland, a lawyer and large landowner, gave a third of a league of land to the railroad.

Cleveland settled in Liberty and his home, now a historical landmark, still stands there, operated by the Daughters of the American Revolution. The home, located at 2131 Grand, was built in 1860.

If you're in Cleveland around lunchtime, try the buffet at Boyett's Cafe, long known for its excellent homestyle meals. The homemade pies are especially tasty. And next door to Boyett's is the studio of East Texas watercolorist Ronnie Wells, one of the region's leading artists. Wells is known for his vignettes of East Texas, including wildlife, abandoned churches, backwood sloughs and old sawmills.

Just south of Boyett's Cafe, on U.S. 59, is an cemetery resting in the highway median. Highway engineers tried a few years ago to relocate 14 graves in the cemetery in order to widen the highway, but descendents of the Riggs family were firm. So there it remains--a cemetery in the middle of the highway right-of-way, possibly the only such graveyard in Texas.

About 10 miles west of Cleveland is Hilltop Herb Farm, where the owners not only grow a variety of herbs, but serve unique meals built around specially-prepared vegetables and fruits. It is advisable to call ahead for reservations.

From Cleveland, proceed south on Texas 321, but a few miles out of Cleveland, turn east on Farm Road 163 at Tarkington Prairie, named for Burton Tarkington, who settled here between 1827 and 1843. Tarkington and other settlers fought hostile Indians before finally winning the land and founding a trading center on the old Lynchburg-Nacogdoches road. In the community is the landmark Wells Store, which was built in 1875 by D.W. Proctor and Company and later operated by L.L. Wells. The store served stagecoach traffic on the Lynchburg-Nacogdoches road and has since been restored. A historical marker stands out front.

On 163, continue south until you come to the intersection of Farm Road 1008, which will carry you through the Kenefick community and into Dayton, a town that straddles another early trade route, the Old Spanish Road, linking Houston and Beaumont. The Day family gave the town its present name, which evolved from Day's Town.

From Dayton, follow U.S. 90 back to Liberty.

(For information about places on this Sunday Drive, contact the Liberty-Dayton Chamber of Commerce, 1915 Trinity Street, Liberty, TX 77575, telephone 409/336-5736, or the Cleveland Chamber of Commerce, 222 S. Bonham Avenue, Box 1733, Cleveland, TX 77327, telephone 409/592-8786.)

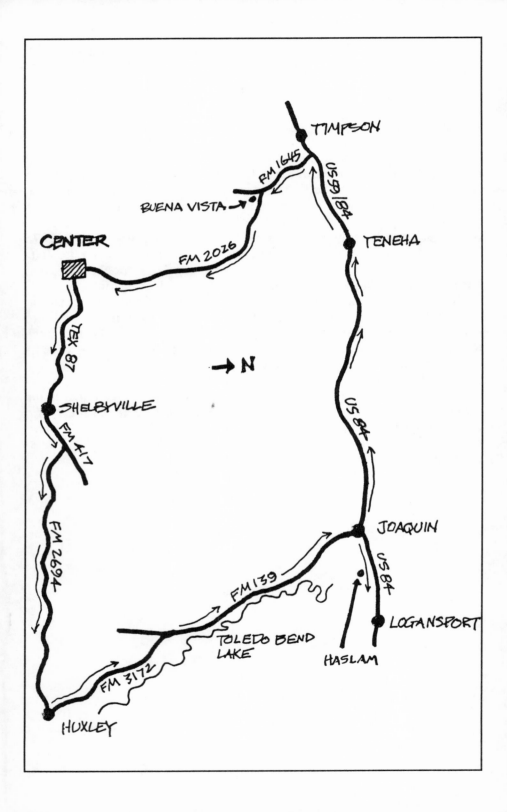

Center:

Land of Teneha, Timpson, Bobo and Blair.

Here's a Sunday Drive with an interesting mix of attractions—country and western music, a sawmill ghost town, an unusual courthouse, one of the biggest lakes in the South, and some excellent down-home meals.

Let's start at Center, the county seat of Shelby County where you'll find one of the last thriving courthouse squares in East Texas—a cluster of businesses lined up on four streets facing an 1885 courthouse of Irish castle design, the only surviving example of this style of architecture in the United States. The courthouse is still a working seat of justice, but visitors are welcome to roam through its ancient hallways.

Spend some time on the square. You'll find quaint gift shops, oldtime hardware stores, and one of the best cheeseburgers in all of East Texas. The magnificent double-meat burger is served at the John C. Rogers Drug Store; don't leave Center until you try it. And, on another side of the town square, a few doors from the local movie theater, you'll find some of the best homemade pies at a cafe known as the Garden Spot. Be sure to try the caramel pie.

Center also boats an excellent rural museum, the Shelby County Museum, with a good collection of farm tools, firearms, antiques and other memorabilia.

From Center, head southeast on U.S. 87 to Shelbyville. A few miles out of town, look for a state historical marker marking the last battle of the Regulators-Moderators War, representing one of the bloodiest eras in East Texas history. The war was characterized by shootings, hangings and clashes until Sam Houston, president of the Republic of Texas, sent in the militia to arrest the leaders of the two factions; they were later forced to negotiate a peace.

At Shelbyville, turn east on Farm Road 417, where you'll start a route that takes you through the Sabine National Forest and some of the prettiest timberlands in Texas. A few miles out of Shelbyville, veer to the right on Farm Road 2694, which will carry you to Boles Field, home of the only dog cemetery in East Texas. Some of the South's best known foxhounds are buried here in a small plot beside the highway.

Continue on Farm Road 2694 until it intersects with Farm Road 3172 at Huxley, which will carry you north alongside Toledo Bend Lake, the largest man-made reservoir in the South. The lake covers 185,000 acres on the Texas-Louisiana border and has more than 650 miles of shoreline. The lake is accessible at several points along this farm road.

If you remain on 3172 and Farm Road 139, you'll eventually wind up at Joaquin on U.S. 84 near the north end of the lake. Take a right on 84 and start toward Logansport, La., and you'll pass through Haslam, a ghost town built in the 1920s by the Pickering Lumber Company. The buildings will be found on the right side of the highway, just across the railroad tracks.

Back at Joaquin, head west on 84 toward Teneha and you'll find yourself in the heart of "Teneha, Timpson, Bobo and Blair." This old diceplayer's chant was made famous by movie cowboy/singer Tex Ritter, who grew up in this part of East Texas.

"Teneha, Timpson, Bobo and Blair," the universal plea for a crap-shooter trying for 10, was started by railroad conductors calling out the four stops on the old Houston, East and West Texas Railroad, and picked up by soldiers marching off to serve their country. During World War II, the phrase was echoed by crapshooters all over the world.

Timpson and Teneha are established towns on U.S. 84 while Bobo and Blair are tiny settlements sometimes overlooked. Bobo is marked only by a sign on U.S. 84 and Blair is remembered only by a church and a cemetery beside FM 2141.

At Timpson, turn south on FM 1645. At the intersection of 1645 and FM 2026 is the old town of Buena Vista, today remembered only by a cemetery. Joseph Burns settled the town in the 1840s with a league and a labor of land he received for soldiering duties with the U.S. Army in its war with Mexico in 1846-48. He laid out a townsite and name it Buena Vista—"a beautiful view"—for a town in Mexico where he fought a battle. The town was also known as Buck Snort, a name that came about when a large buck walked into the middle of the settlement and snorted defiantly.

With the arrival of the Houston, East and West Texas Railroad in the 1880s, most of Buena Vista's stores were relocated at Timpson, four miles west of the town, and at Teneha, six miles east, both on the new railroad line.

At the Buena Vista Cemetery, take FM 2026 and follow it through the settlements of Prospect and Folsom back into Center to complete your Sunday Drive.

(For more information about the places found on this Sunday Drive, contact the Center Chamber of Commerce, 321 Shelbyville, Center, TX 75935, telephone 409/598-3682.)